# THE ANTIRACIST EDUCATOR

This struggle may be a moral one, or it may be a physical one, and it may be both moral and physical, but it must be a struggle. Power concedes nothing without a demand. It never did and it never will. Find out just what any people will quietly submit to and you have found out the exact measure of injustice and wrong which will be imposed upon them, and these will continue till they are resisted with either words or blows, or with both.

Frederick Douglass

# PRANAV PATEL

# THE ANTIRACIST EDUCATOR

CORWIN

Los Angeles | London | New Delhi
Singapore | Washington DC | Melbourne

SAGE Publications Ltd
1 Oliver's Yard
55 City Road
London EC1Y 1SP

CORWIN
A SAGE company
2455 Teller Road
Thousand Oaks, California 91320
(0800)233-9936
www.corwin.com

SAGE Publications India Pvt Ltd
B 1/I 1 Mohan Cooperative Industrial Area
Mathura Road
New Delhi 110 044

SAGE Publications Asia-Pacific Pte Ltd
3 Church Street
#10-04 Samsung Hub
Singapore 049483

Editor: Delayna Spencer
Senior assistant editor: Catriona McMullen
Production editor: Katherine Haw
Indexer: Martin Hargreaves
Marketing manager: Dilhara Attygalle
Cover design: Wendy Scott
Typeset by: Knowledgeworks Global Ltd.
Printed in the UK

**Library of Congress Control Number:
2021943033**

**British Library Cataloguing in Publication data**

A catalogue record for this book is available from the
British Library

ISBN 978-1-5297-6736-0
ISBN 978-1-5297-6735-3 (pbk)

At SAGE we take sustainability seriously. Most of our products are printed in the UK using responsibly
sourced papers and boards. When we print overseas we ensure sustainable papers are used as measured
by the PREPS grading system. We undertake an annual audit to monitor our sustainability.

# Contents

## About the Author

Pranav Patel is an educator with nearly two decades of experience across primary, secondary and higher education. As a member of the global majority, he has been a witness to the impact of oppression through his work with students, as a teacher and a leader. Pranav's commitment and sustained work towards greater equity is long-standing – for him, change comes from action, and now is the time to act.

## Acknowledgements

Thanking every single soul that has come before me. I do not walk on this Earth alone but with the power of resistance through the endurance and persistence of our ancestors. Specifically, this book and I exist because of my father, Amrutlal Chhotubhai Patel, and his continuous commitment to justice.

To my family with whom I may not share a blood line. You have always walked shoulder to shoulder alongside me and I hope you continue to shout loudly and ask defiantly for nothing less than parity from all of society. To Gareth Robinson and Michael Dayhar I genuinely wouldn't be the man I am without your support and love.

I have to thank Imane Maghrani for extending my thinking to beyond where I thought my mind and soul could venture; for keeping me going while traversing North London's parks, Sarif Alrai and my editor Delayna Spencer, who is part of the reason I actually got to the end.

During the writing of this book Ruth Lillis, Maryellen McGrath, T'Challa Greaves, Penny Rabiger, Di Leedham, Kay Sidebottom, Elena Kkama, Louise Pennington, Sarah Britton, Alison Kriel, Róisín Byrne, Mehmet Ali Ahmet, Rosie Mellors, Sukhvinder Ubhi and countless others, you have all held space and my physical body in ways I can't even begin to describe.

Credit has to go to each and every person who has subjected my melanated kin and I to acts of violence, whether physical, verbal or epistemic, to all the folx who are used to the 'I don't see colour', 'I have black friends and family' and other racist narratives, not forgetting those who have engaged in white solidarity, the white saviour complex, utilised and acted on white women's tears, and propagated and championed the damage of an ethnocentric curriculum. Thank you. You have made my voice louder and my arms stronger.

Finally. I say this loudly, proudly and clearly and so should you.

I demand a better world.

Let Ganesh lead these words.

# Introduction to Antiracism for Teachers

At a time like this, scorching Irony, not convincing argument, is needed. O! had I the ability, and could reach the nation's ear, I would, to-day, pour out a fiery stream of biting ridicule, blasting reproach, withering sarcasm, and stern rebuke. For it is not light that is needed, but fire; it is not the gentle shower, but thunder. We need the storm, the whirlwind, and the earthquake. The feeling of the nation must be quickened; the conscience of the nation must be roused; the propriety of the nation must be startled; the hypocrisy of the nation must be exposed; and its crimes against God and man must be proclaimed and denounced. (Frederick Douglass, in Foner, 1999, p. x)

## Introduction

Welcome, folx. You've picked up a book designed to make you feel uncomfortable, to challenge your thinking and to make your practice and environment a fairer place. Common responses to this type of work include anger, tears, wanting to walk away and sometimes, threats of violence. It's okay if you experience those feelings. I want you to remember that these feelings are defence mechanisms which stem from the systems and structures of our society. This book is not about you, but that society. The structures that our society are built upon means that there are people who are oppressed, and others who actively benefit from that as a direct result. For this to end, we must face up to the fact that we all have a role in racial equity and must take an active part in fighting injustice in our society.

Racism is often defined solely as acts of physical violence and the use of derogatory terms towards People of Colour. Although violence and words are used within racism, these actions should be seen as symptoms of a greater issue. Racism comes in four forms: **Individual**, **Institutional**, **Systemic**, **Internalised**.

In this book, we will mainly concentrate on systemic and institutionalised racism. Within school systems, these two forms of racism are the most active and pervasive. Together, we will look at how our actions, ideologies, and thoughts uphold a society in which the journeys of People of Colour are fundamentally different from those of white people.

## Systematic and Institutional Racism

In describing society, let us use the analogy of a house. Individual racism is analogous to the violence (whether verbal or physical) that takes place in a room in the house. The impacts of individualised acts of hate are abhorrent. As a Man of Colour, I have experienced these frequently, and as a result, I am well-versed in the damage they can inflict. These acts stem from more ubiquitous structures that provide the impetus for that hate. The allegory stretches to having a hole in the ceiling, which damages the contents of the room. The leak is not produced or caused by the room's contents but is a symptom of structural issues in the roof.

In our analogy, institutionalised or organisational racism are the rules of the house, which include who can enter which rooms, who can sit at the table, eat at the table, speak at the table, how decisions are made in the house, and so on. I am assuming many of you are asking, 'How do our organisations propagate racism?' This is because each school in the UK is part of a wider societal structure that upholds this propagation. By the end of this book you may be better versed to recognise this.

Systemic racism is pernicious in its very nature, but it is the proverbial foundations of society and the foundation of our house; taking it even further, it is the fact that our 'house' exists at all. It is essential for us to recognise that racism is not just who we are; instead, in understanding systemic racism, we must realise the structures and walls within which we reside dictate the outcomes for millions of people.

First, let us accept that systemic racism impacts People of Colour and simultaneously does not and cannot have the same effect on white people.

Yes, I am saying that white people cannot be victims of systemic racism.

On the face of it, this may sound unfair.

Come with me here.

Imagine that I, Pran Patel, hate white people (I do not), and in my relative position of power in schools, I refuse to employ white applicants. Think about the consequences. Would this be unfair? Yes, absolutely. Are the white applicants facing an instance of discrimination? Yes. But what happens tomorrow? Those very same individuals apply to any other organisation and are faced with a fair opportunity and an advantage. Nothing, in essence, changes for those racialised as white; the architecture of the system itself is designed by and for them. However, there are obvious stark barriers and differences when considering Teachers of Colour.

[BAME]¹ teachers are, on average, paid less than their peers, commonly face discrimination and prejudice when applying for jobs or promotion and typically face both overt and covert racism in the workplace. (Keates, 2021)

Racial prejudice and discrimination are different entities although they are often conflated. An easy way of defining them is that racial prejudice is based around prejudged attitudes towards a group and discrimination is rooted in the actions that stem from those attitudes. Racism, whether individual, institutionalised or systemic, should be seen as a consequence of the earth on which we built our house. The roots of oppression start with the fact we have inherited this land after a legacy of exploitation and theft. For centuries Brown and Black bodies, lands and resources have been fair game in the hunt for power.

The esteemed Jamaican philosopher Charles W. Mills takes Jean-Jacques Rousseau's work and filters it through a much-needed racial lens. The basis of Rousseau's social contract is that individuals willingly give up some of their civil freedoms and submit to authority in return for protection of their remaining rights and thus maintain the status quo. What have we given up to enjoy these freedoms? Make no mistake, our racial contract is written in the blood of the 'other' and on the scraps and remains of our collective conscience. Those who came before us sacrificed their morality to guarantee that they were assured those freedoms and accepted slavery, colonisation and murder as a consequence.

To ensure that we accepted and continue to accept these horrific practices, society offers a range of distraction methods.

## 'But I'm not racist'

The words 'Racist' and 'White Supremacy' to the majority of people will conjure the more extreme images of the Ku Klux Klan and burning crosses, or swastikas and concentration camps. Due to this, there is often a shutdown reaction of 'No, I'm not', 'You don't know me', 'How is that racist?' or 'That is not what I meant' if someone is confronted as having done or said something racist. It's easy to ignore our own complicity in a system when we hold these as extreme exemplars. However, we don't need to don a hood or march with burning torches in order to perpetuate harm to People of Colour.

I acknowledge that being called racist is hard and hurtful; it might go against the perception you hold of yourself. However, together we need to consider the wider picture here: being called a 'racist' is far easier than facing systemic racism daily. We have to accept that our actions can and will uphold white supremacy. We can all do racist things but not necessarily be a 'racist'; yet, the damage caused is the same even if the intentions are not.

**Figure 1.1** The good to bad, not racist to racist binary

When a Person of Colour labels, points or calls your actions out as being racist or upholding white supremacy, the primary response should always be to listen and be ready to learn. Whether you believe it's true or not, as a white person, doesn't matter at all, you're being told by someone who experiences this every day that your actions are not okay.

The poles of good and bad are often mapped against the 'not racist' and 'racist' binary. The existence of this false dipole is the source of this offence. The notion that our actions and beliefs directly influence our personal social morality and buy us a one-way ticket to heaven or hell is where the problem lies. Here I would be remiss if I didn't mention that 'not racist' doesn't really exist.

> What's the problem with being 'not racist'? It is a claim that signifies neutrality: 'I am not a racist, but neither am I aggressively against racism.' But there is no neutrality in the racism struggle. The opposite of 'racist' isn't 'not racist.' It is 'anti-racist.' (Kendi, 2019, p. 9)

Even if 'not racist' was a stance that we could aspire to, is that a label we truly want to adopt? I am often told 'I'm not racist, what has any of this got to do with me? This is other people's problem, Pran'. The 'not racist' rhetoric implies that you have done your bit, racism has ended. Hooray! If you accept that systemic racism exists, and it certainly does, then it will continue to exist whether you refuse to actively engage in it or not, which means by being not racist you leave society firmly where it stands.

## Racist to Antiracist Spectrum

Let's look at the racist to antiracist spectrum. The racist end of the spectrum is broadly split into these six categories:

Apathy
Minimisation
Concealed racism
Discrimination
Violence and calls for violence
Murder

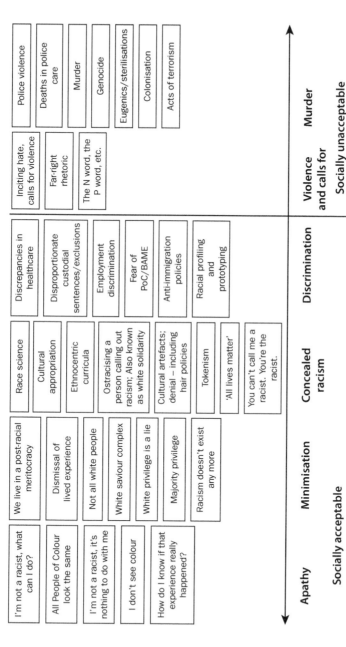

**Figure 1.2** Racism: socially acceptable to socially unacceptable spectrum

To start with, let's look at the 'colour blind' ideology. There is a misconception that the 'I don't see colour' label falls on the side of antiracism. I understand that many people have been sold this lie by the wilful appropriation of Dr Martin Luther King's work (or I should say cherry-picked epigrams from his work). When we choose not to judge by the colour of skin we must not also erase the life experiences that come with that very same melanin. (Colour blind as a term is problematic when we look through an ableist lens: being any sort of blind does not inhibit a person's ability to observe at all. I recognise the use of this language because I felt it is important to highlight the problematic nature of the common phrase.)

As a small (Brown) child, I once visited the doctor about a small dark patch of skin. He assessed and responded softly, 'There was an infection there once but it is gone now. Remember that your skin is special, it remembers through the mark that it survived and this is the way it tells the world how brave it was.' The lives of People of Colour are very different to the lives of white folx; we wear our experiences and journeys in the colour of our skin. As a Man of Colour, I have personally experienced those patches and marks through physical, verbal, emotional violence and seen time and time again people who look like me go through the same experiences. When erasing people's right to being observed by their colour you deny the trials that they face and a fundamental part of themselves.

In addition, the notion that any person can act in a fashion where there is no recognition of race is a neurological and cultural fallacy. Our brains are simply not designed like that. Even if you were the bearer of this mythical power it does nothing to stop the systemic, institutional or even individual racism People of Colour face every day. You may be reading this thinking that I am being overly harsh in my tone. You may feel that people are trying their best and they are acting in good faith. In this case, good intentions truly pave the road to hell. I cannot say this enough. White people's intentions and feelings may be at the heart of racism but they are not at the centre of antiracism's story.

White people often feel like they are judged unfairly when they commit microaggressions, engage in white saviourism, white fragility or white solidarity because after all they didn't mean any harm by it. Let's concentrate on that word 'harm'. People of Colour are harmed by these acts, systemically, institutionally and individually. Does the intention ever impact on the recovery time of being struck? Does it soften the blow? Make the attacks less frequent and consistent? If anything, all those intentions do is simply make the impact of that violence sting for a little bit longer. Harm is harm regardless of intent. Let's just get over ourselves and first concentrate on repairing the damage and then attempt to stop continuing with it.

# White Supremacy

The pyramid of white supremacy adapted by Ellen Tuzzolo (2016) originally created by Safehouse Progressive Alliance for Nonviolence (2005) is an inverted form of the spectrum. This version of the taxonomy is particularly useful as I envision it as a physical entity. Removing or minimising layers makes the structure fall apart; the layers are consequential and cumulative – without any one of the sections the pyramid loses shape and the racism loses power. This pyramid is not saying that you as an individual will go from indifference to mass murder. What it highlights is the structures those extreme actions are built upon and also the capacity that you have to make changes at the bottom which will topple the higher layers.

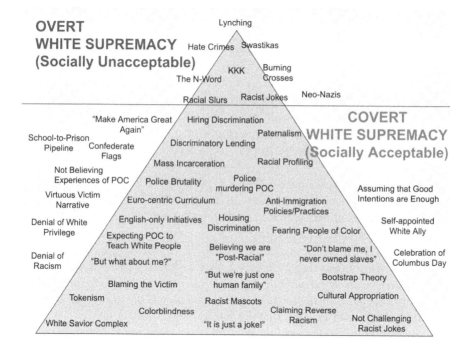

**Figure 1.3** Pyramid of white supremacy

*Source*: Ellen Tuzzolo adapted from Safehouse Progressive Alliance for Nonviolence (SPAN) www.safehousealliance.org

The first four sections of the pyramid are (from the bottom up):

- Indifference
- Minimisation
- Veiled racism
- Discrimination

All of these are, in the main, socially acceptable. Let that sink in. The majority of actions that are on the racist side of the spectrum are unlikely to be recognised by a bystander; it is only when explicit violence begins that people begin to resist.

The above may come as a bitter pill, it certainly did for me. Yes, I am admitting that I spent most of my past and some of my present undertaking actions that exist on the lower tiers of the pyramid. Let us all hold our fragility together. Believe me when I say: 'I too promote a systemically racist societal status quo and I also benefit from that very same status quo.'

I am a Person of Colour suggesting that I uphold the same systems of white supremacy. Yes, you read that correctly. When interrogating that statement further it makes perfect sense: how could I not uphold those same systems? I have been educated, socialised and acculturated in a society that disadvantages People of Colour in real terms and across all sectors; I have been trained to see this as the norm for the best part of four decades.

How did I feel when I realised that I have benefited from these systems of oppression? My moment came through a torrent of realisations. As a Brown man I have encountered overt and implicit racism within the education profession at every juncture on the way. When I became a senior leader, I sat in my office and reflected on the obstacles I overcame and the blood, sweat and tears that had gone into gaining this prize. Revelling in the victorious moment of crossing the line. And then it hit me like a slap in the face and I actually mouthed the words: 'Wait there... Hold up... if I were a Black man, a Woman of Colour, this journey would've been more difficult... if I were trans Woman of Colour ...'.

For that moment I was shocked, I physically reeled back in my wheelie chair, and I remember feeling the need to resist this dissonance because on some level I wanted to defend myself: 'I worked really hard.' I was protecting the notion that I deserved all that I had achieved and it was solely down to my hard work. This is the source of much of the resistance to equity, fear that an unfair system means that we are not good enough and that we did not earn all that we have.

Another side to this is that as a cis gendered man, I benefit from society's patriarchal structures; it is difficult to own that I live in a world where I accept that, because of cis men (through our actions or inaction/ silence), the lives of women, trans, non-binary, and people of all other genders are made worse. If I openly accept that this is wrong, I have to then consequently accept that this is and has been okay by me because, after all, I have and continue to benefit from this imbalance. The easiest option is for me to deny its existence, through distraction, silence and flight. I get the need to run, I understand the fragility that recognition brings; however, if we care about fairness, we really need to get over ourselves as a starting point. These feelings and subsequent actions are defined by Dr Robin Di Angelo as 'white fragility': 'These moves include the outward display of emotions such as anger, fear, and guilt, and behaviours such as **argumentation**, **silence**, and **leaving the stress-inducing situation**. These behaviours, in turn, function to reinstate white racial equilibrium' (Di Angelo, 2011, p. 54).

To move towards the antiracist pole, whether systemically or personally, takes effort and work. Antiracism is not a fad, a course, or a tick box exercise. At the risk of putting people off, you should be aware that once you put in the effort it becomes even harder. The very nature of the status quo means we all have the tendency to fail to meet its standards constantly. Forget the wicked, there is no rest for the **antiracist**.

## What Can I Do?

Antiracism is an ideology which aims to change the norm. For centuries People of Colour have been oppressed by systems and structures which have served to denigrate their rights. It is easy to pretend that the need for an antiracism movement is isolated to cases of police brutality in a far-away land of the not so free; however, this is the very tip of the iceberg and antiracists are the ice picks chipping away at it.

> The only way to undo racism is to consistently identify and describe it – and then dismantle it. (Kendi, 2019)

The curricula we are taught as young people is the starting point for the way we view the world (our ontology) and the way we gather and accept knowledge (our epistemology). As educators, the acknowledgement of the lenses on our day-to-day practice is critical, and their impact is not solely isolated to our own lives, as through the nature of our roles we continue to protect and propagate those lenses, affecting our students. Are you as an educator complicit in that daily oppression? How do we, in the words of Dr Ibram X. Kendi, consistently 'identify, describe and dismantle racism'? How do we challenge the racist structures in which we were brought up, taught by our own teachers and now continue to propagate? As educators, this process begins with us looking inwards to our actions and our complicity.

### Reflection

Here are some questions I would like you to reflect on before reading on:

1.  Do you treat all students fairly?
2.  In which ways do you change their lives?
3.  Do you teach students to recognise systems and empower them to act to promote or resist them democratically?

It is important to recognise that we have all gone through the same education systems, live in the same society and thus have experienced the same inculcation which has led us to our systemically racist present. This personal recognition and identification may elicit fragility, but it is important to evaluate what is at stake. Ultimately this comes down to a balance of your personal offence and feelings being more important than the experiences and the future experiences of the students we serve. People always look for the 'what to do', the 'how to' and a step-by-step guide. This part of your journey is not a tick box checklist and is a lifelong commitment. It starts with an introspection which seeks changes to the self and then constant re-evaluation of our role with regards to the whole.

## The Journey

Here, I want to highlight different stages of the journey you will experience in your movement towards the antiracist end of the spectrum. This is a consequential process only in so far as to say that the stages cannot be skipped, people may be moved both forwards and backwards and straddle the categories through their lifetime.

### Unawareness

This is the stage where many people start. Here, there is an assumption that race doesn't matter, and we have no idea of the privileges and power structures intertwined in the systematic nature of our society.

Common phrases and thoughts:

- Racism? That doesn't happen here.
- We ended racism centuries ago.

### Blame

Here, we begin to realise that inequalities exist in society, which impact People of Colour. This point of the journey is fraught with anxiety and people start to seek relief, sometimes by placing the blame at the door of the victims. The dissonance from the last stage can be overpowering and the natural response is to resist it through more deflection and blame.

Common phrases and thoughts:

- Why do People of Colour always make everything about race?
- Be more like us (white people) – that will mean less racism. Don't be too different – that's taking it too far. We can accept differences as long as those people assimilate.

- This is all about me, I can change myself and be 'not racist'.
- If 'they' just did/did not do X then 'they' would have no problem with racism.
- We live in a meritocracy – People of Colour don't work hard enough.
- People of Colour choose not to work and expect a leg up.

## Light-bulb moment

This is where acceptance occurs and the realities of our society come into focus. However, the struggle against racism can appear so huge a task that people can fall back to blame in order to lift the feelings of futility.

Common phrases and thoughts:

- I/We live in a racist society and I am part of that problem.
- I'm paralysed by guilt/shame/helplessness; there is nothing I can do.

## Responsibility

This may sound like the promised land; people are ready to take personal responsibility! However, this is fraught with danger as the responsibility is often seen as individual and so centres on the individual. Here the tendency is to shout about diversity but not tackle the issues which caused the non-representation in the first place.

Common phrases and thoughts:

- I am working hard on diversity.
- The system works but we just need to help minorities get into those positions.
- I'm here to save People of Colour.

## Action

The real work begins here. We move from an individual approach to a collective lens. As a Brown man I may not exhibit anti-Blackness but it is inherent in the South Asian diaspora and, as I make up part of the whole, this is my responsibility. As I am British and a member of society my actions are secondary to the society I uphold.

Common phrases and thoughts:

- I'm struggling with both benefiting from and attacking the same system.

- It's not about tolerating people.
- Diversity is a false win; we shouldn't expect people to conform if they have value already.

## Resistance

Resistance is the goal. All action is collective, strategic and impactful. There is a real acknowledgement that the structures must change to impact on individual, institutional and systemic racism.

Common phrases and thoughts:

- Where is my role in this change?
- Is there a way I can lift the voices of People of Colour?
- I can change my own actions.
- I seek to change the thoughts of my leaders.
- How do we strategise to make change?

# Common Arguments and Misconceptions Against Antiracism

## We Live in a Meritocracy

People believe that we live in a fair society where one can progress based on their merit. If this is true, why do our leaders, CEOs, professors and so on always look the same? Why are so many of our school leaders and teachers white? The highest performing group at undergraduate level is that within the Asian subset, yet where are they represented in the academy? Indeed, Black students have high numbers at undergraduate level, and yet there are only 155 Black university professors out of 18,770 employed by universities in the UK (HESA, 2021).

The meritocracy in its entirety is a racist construct. If you believe that success is predicated on effort then looking at the world around us it seems that having melanated skin means that people don't work hard enough. This, of course, leads to the same old racist tropes. The meritocracy also feeds into our apparent efforts to redress the balance in our society. This false narrative leads back to unfairness. If we live in a world which is predicated on merit, it follows that we should provide everyone with exactly the same resources to achieve. This is commonly known as the struggle towards equality.

In our classrooms, giving and treating all pupils the same still leads to disproportionate outcomes. Equality should not be the aim, but rather an equitable response depends on each pupil and their relative position in society. If some folx have already started ahead of others, giving every participant a 10m advantage in a sprint does not make the competition fairer. We will explore through this book how race impacts almost every facet of education and how treating pupils the same actually reinforces this cyclical journey of prejudice and discrimination.

## 'It was a different time, people did things differently then'

When analysing texts or events in history, antiracists are often told that they are holding people from the past to account by today's standards. I would agree, that we are holding people to account against today's standards of moral decency but that metric has always existed. To claim, 'everyone accepted slavery as that was the standard' erases the voices of the oppressed. It silences the voices of the enslaved peoples and proposes that they don't count as everyone or anyone. Were their opinions not as valid? Were they not as human or human at all?

## This is Left Wing, Anti-Capitalist and Extremist

There is an element to antiracism that criticises capitalism as an economic policy, and there is no hiding this. The system was built on the subjugation of People of Colour, and this is still arguably the case. This is often used to dismiss movements that challenge the status quo. We would do well to remember that it is the role of academics and educators to critique society and to encourage critical thinking skills in those that they teach. The horizontal political axis of left and right is based solely on an economic ideology, and I struggle to see what that has to do with treating people fairly? Remember, you can be a free-market fundamentalist and accept antiracism, and equally, you can be a libertarian socialist and still not appear on the antiracist side of the spectrum.

## 'Antiracist teaching doesn't have a place in the classroom'

Recently there has been high-profile push-back against well-established academic subjects like whiteness studies and critical race theory. Common arguments against well-defined sociological structures such as white privilege are often levelled in the realms of truth with demands of evidence. All structures in the social sciences do not and cannot deliver definite truths like the natural sciences. If you are still not convinced, remember everything in our own profession of education cannot deliver an 'absolute truth'.

Even the most ardent opponents of antiracism in education are still advocates of critical thinking. Without the safe environment of a classroom setting to introduce these concepts, how can any of us claim to be educators, purveyors of knowledge and skills? Antiracist education seeks to open the eyes of our students to analyse their community and ultimately become better citizens of the world. If we are not enabling our students to be better, and create a better world, then what truly, I ask, is our purpose?

## Conclusion

You have started on the road towards an antiracist classroom. There will be times on this journey that you will question yourself, the world around you and even the tarmac you walk upon. The starting position is always met with tentative awareness. We work in a system which upholds racism. Ultimately, we are all complicit and responsible in that world.

Of the four types of racism, we will pay passing attention to individual and internalised forms in this book, as they are consequential and symptoms of systemic and institutionalised racism. There may be times you question yourself, society or the world while you are reading. Remember racism hides within the good person and bad person dichotomy. To 'uphold' is a verb; we may all uphold white supremacy without being a 'bad' person or being a 'racist'. Our personal thoughts and feelings should take a back seat in the classroom; this is about building a fairer world for all of our students.

This ride is not and will not be easy. Expect fragility and be ready for the resistance.

### Chapter Takeaways

- Racism is embedded in every aspect/structure of our society; for this reason it is impossible to be automatically antiracist.
- Non-racism is a form of neutrality whereas antiracism requires action.
- We are all upholding white supremacy, and this includes myself.
- Question where on the antiracist to racist spectrum you fall and what you can do to remove a layer from the pyramid of white supremacy.
- All of the above will impact on your practice as a teacher and an educational leader; spend some time reflecting on how it already does.

### Note

[1] BAME is Black, Asian and minority ethnic.

# Teacher Bias and the Damage of Stereotyping

Bias and prejudice are attitudes to be kept in hand, not attitudes to be avoided. (Charles Curtis, first US Vice President of Colour, 1929–1933, and member of the Kaw Nation)

## Introduction

Many teachers may feel it is impossible for them or their colleagues to have racial biases against their students. That racism is compiled as a list of acts that happen elsewhere. Some folx will even recognise that racism exists in education but not in the teachers around them, the mysterious nebulous process of having systemic racism without any single educator contributing to it.

In this chapter we will look at teachers' racial biases starting with the source of the systemic impact on students. Stereotypes are formed through group assumptions which are then reinforced. These biases have a dual impact on students' sense of self and their position in this world through a variety of socio-psychological phenomena which directly impact on outcomes for Students of Colour.

## What Is the Source of Bias?

Why do labels exist? Where or what is the need to ascribe to a group? People tend to form groups because of a need for safety, after all, we feel more protected with people who believe the same things as us. Collectives are found in every facet of our lives, from our families (we proudly show off our surnames as a consequence) to our sports affiliations.

I grew up in the Black Country, a small area in between the cities of Wolverhampton and Birmingham, about equidistant from two football clubs, Wolverhampton Wanderers and West Bromwich Albion. My family already had allegiances to the 'Wolves' for a variety of reasons, so I pitched my flag firmly with the Wanderers. I grew up in a personal environment where our club was bolstered, its achievements were widely celebrated and almost everything to do with football was framed through a lens of sainthood when it came to the Wolves. Those associated with the club, whether players, staff or other bodies, could do no wrong.

Being a football fan or part of any group brings a sense of safety and belonging. After all, a group of people with a common badge have a joint vision of something to hope for, fight for and protect each other for as a consequence. My football club and my fellow supporters feel like a family. Our successes are my successes and our failures are also my failures. Living under a Wolves banner means that no one is going to attack you for your choice of football team within that group. People group together because this breeds a sense of belonging and where people belong they feel safe. On the flip side, the impact of being inculcated into a world of gold and black (Wolverhampton Wanderers' colours) had and has implications for my perception of the world.

---

## Reflection

1. Does your school foster this sense of belonging?
2. Who are the students that seems to buy into the school and its sense of belonging?
3. Which groups of students regularly reject the idea?

---

When people form collectives they tend to use pronouns and adjectives like 'us', 'we' and 'our'. There is an actual internalisation of a group of people with common characteristics and/or beliefs and this has its sociological advantages. The reason division is necessary is because of the very nature of the collectives and their need to exist. All members of a collective fall under the same overall vision – all Wolves fans want our club to 'do well' but on the individual level there will be varying examples of these outcomes. For example, for some fans winning at all costs is acceptable, but for others, like myself, the quality of the football is our specific measure of success.

> The purpose of a social collective is to elevate their visions as true, denigrate others as false and/or to subjugate others; without those functions the idea would be meaningless and vain. (Von Mises, 2003, p. 43)

Left unchecked, the differentiation between personal visions can lead to in-fighting, sedition, and ultimately mutiny. The way collectives are kept together is through the idea of the 'decency principle' – Why would you not want to be part of our collective when we are all decent people? Why would you want to be part of the other? The consequential step then is that collectives create heroes within their 'us' and villains that inhabit the 'them', so, in the case of West Midlands football, 'the other' is a neighbouring club, West Bromwich Albion.

## How Do We Differentiate Between the Us and the Other?

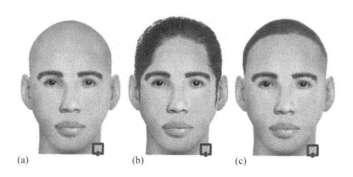

(a)                          (b)                          (c)

**Figure 2.1**   The same race effect. (a) Ambiguous-race face is missing the facial marker (hair). When a Hispanic hairstyle is added to this ambiguous-race face, the face is perceived as 'Hispanic' (b). When an Afro hairstyle is added to the ambiguous-race face, the face is perceived as 'Black' (c).

*Source*: MacLin, O. H. and Malpass, R. S. (2003). The ambiguous-race face illusion. *Perception*, 32(2): 249–252. doi:10.1068/p5046. Republished with permission of SAGE Publications.

MacLin et al. (2001) and MacLin and Malpass (2003) investigated the cross-race face-recognition deficit. They took a computer-generated racially ambiguous face (a) and added an overlay of hairstyles from traditionally Latinx and African American communities. They found that people who belong to either 'race' were more likely to recognise the (identical) face more readily when the hair overlay corresponded to their own. This impact on recognition and recall is due to the categorisation components on our brains. We believe that faces are recognised across various axes of metrics such as nose width, eye size, and so on. When the face of someone from another 'race' is presented, it is put into an 'other' category which means that it is processed differently from those metrics.

The fact that what our brains observe is dependent on the perception of 'race' may come as no surprise. This process is natural: in Figure 2.2 each 'Mach' band looks darker to its left and lighter to its right, although they are all solid boxes of a uniform colour. The effect is caused through the difference of the information of the other colours in its environment. Remove the other strips with your hands and see for yourself.

Researchers Levin and Banaji (2006) cite the diagram in their paper entitled 'Distortions in the perceived lightness of faces: The role of race

**Figure 2.2**  Mach bands in which a series of bands appear to be lighter on the right and darker on the left because of contrast with the darker bands on the right and lighter bands on the left.

*Source*: Levin, D. T. and Banaji, M. R. (2006). Distortions in the perceived lightness of faces: The role of race categories. *Journal of Experimental Psychology: General*, 135(4): 501–512. Reprinted with permission under the STM publisher's organisation.

categories'. In this paper they look at the perception of colour based on facial features. Here they conclude that perception of lightness of people should include broad contextual and knowledge-based influences as the current emphasis is solely on the surface properties. Perceptions of colour, tone and recognition are dependent more on the wavelengths of light that are reflected from the object. I have used the diagram reproduced as Figure 2.3 in thousands of workshops, and the question which comes with the slide is 'Which one of these people has the darkest skin?'

Even though I know the answer, that they are all the same colour, my brain sees the face on the left as being darker. With those facial features present the brain associates and categorises and fills in the rest.

Black      Ambiguous      White

**Figure 2.3**  Which one of these people has the darkest skin?

*Source*: Levin, D. T. and Banaji, M. R. (2006). Distortions in the perceived lightness of faces: The role of race categories. *Journal of Experimental Psychology: General*, 135(4): 501–512. Reprinted with permission under the STM publisher's organisation.

**A**        **B**        **C**

**Figure 2.4**  What impact does the addition of a racialised marker have to perception? Ambiguous race faces. **A** represents a unique face (without the key feature hair); **B** represents a unique face + Hispanic hairstyle; and **C** represents a unique face + African American hairstyle.

*Source*: MacLin, O. H. and Malpass, R. S. (2001). Reprinted with permission under the STM publisher's organisation.

In a previous study, MacLin and Malpass (2001) found that identical faces with the addition of a typical African American hairstyle were perceived as having a darker complexion than the Hispanic face, with less protruding eyes, and wider mouth/face. When asked about their perceptions of personality of the faces, there were differences in assertiveness, warmth, trustworthiness, strength and tenseness. These identical faces were not only observed to have different physical features but elicited different perceptions about the personality of the owner.

In summary, our brain's perception is not a simple process of your eyes analysing the wavelengths, frequencies and intensities of the light received. The colours in the mach bands and Levin and Banaji's diagram show us that this is dependent on the environment and a history of reference. MacLin and Malpass (2001) found that our perception of faces through a legacy of associations changes not only our visual perception of colour and race but also evaluations of friendliness, aggressiveness and danger, or the lack thereof. Our society is leaning towards collectives and the collectives which we are taught have value. This is how our brain processes the world around us. While both of these processes are natural and automatic they do create a breeding ground for racism (and other oppressions) to flourish unknowingly and surreptitiously.

## Instant Evaluation

Part of being human is the ability to form and nurture relationships; these essential interactions create the essence of our lives. When meeting a person from any social group, we initially tend to make two simultaneous social evaluations of competence and warmth. Competency as a social value is translated into a gauge for awe about those in the 'in group' and a potential threat when considering a person from a possible 'out group'. This reaction to competence depends on a need to compete for resources, power, or other aspects of social value (Sibley and Osborne, 2015). When meeting a new colleague, we likely ask ourselves: Is this person able to take what is mine? What can they give me and what can I learn from them personally and professionally? The other metric is warmth, a measure of friendliness, trustworthiness, and sociability (Fiske, 2018). It is the intersection of these two positions that leads to any future proceedings of prejudice, interaction and relationship.

---

## ACTIVITY

Take a moment to reflect on your current circle of friends **or** your professional network.

Think about the racial and ethnic group they reside in:

**Table 2.1**   Use this table to interrogate your personal and professional networks

| Friends/Professional Network | Racial and Ethnic Group |
|---|---|
|  |  |
|  |  |
|  |  |
|  |  |

- Of your professional network, think about who you see as the most skilled? Who is the most competent? Who do you rely on?
- Of your friendship group, who do you see as being the friendliest and warmest? Who do you rely on?

Now, think about what racial/ethnic group the people you have categorised belong to.

Do you notice any patterns? What is the racial make-up of the group? How do you perceive each person?

| Case Study: Being Othered |
| --- |

Jenny comes to school full of energy. She has had a wonderful day and is unbelievably proud of the work she has done and is pleased to receive praise from her teachers. She is a diligent student learning the humble ways of school.

Jamal is a melanated male student with exactly the same traits. While walking into school Jenny is complimented on her new jacket, 'she looks really smart'. Jamal is sneered at and told to remove his new hoodie as he enters the building (he was going to take it off anyway).

Walking the corridor Jenny is full of beans, she is a charismatic child and she's playful and excitable with her group of friends. Jamal spends his time in 'gangs' of boys; they bound up and down the corridor like they own the place, pushing and bouncing off each other.

…

Jenny is outraged at the injustice of the removal of hair ribbons. She makes a stand, she refuses to remove the ribbons and every morning is challenged on the school new rule. Jenny is eventually sent to the headteacher to discuss her views and commended on her political discourse. Jamal is wearing his hair in locs with beads, the way his father and forefathers have done for millennia. Jamal sits in an isolation booth, excluded from lessons until his parents meet with the senior leadership team about his flagrant act of defiance.

Jenny is opinionated and sometimes can't control her passion and calls out in class. Jamal is rude and shouts out often. Jenny is working at a stables and supporting various charities with her parents after school and she sometimes misses homework and parents' evenings. Her teachers say that we have to take this into account, education is not just about producing work and she is learning through her experience. Jamal has a part-time job and uses this time to supplement his family income, causing him to miss similar deadlines.

What are the actual differences? There are none. You may not have seen it and you may not continue to see it, but Jamal and scores of other students certainly do and will. The worst part of not having the ability to engage in this awareness is that it is Jamal, not us, who will feel the consequences.

# In Groups, Out Groups and Whiteness

'In groups' are based on people we choose to identify with. The social lens we use with them is often rose-tinted as a result. Taking an everyday lens, the likelihood of people falling into an 'in group' is determined by the perception of their group's proximity to whiteness. Whiteness is not predicated by race; instead, it is a measure of the model traits of those who bear systemic power:

> Whiteness is a hegemonic system that perpetuates certain dominant ide-
> ologies about who receives power and privilege. Whiteness maintains
> itself in cultures through power dynamics within language, religion, class,
> race relations, sexual orientation, etc. (Carter et al., 2007, p. 152)

Differences in power between racial groups have long existed; look at
slavery as the ultimate example of othering. An analysis which is useful
to explain today's power dynamics can be found in Charles Mills' book
*The Racial Contract* (1997), which states that chattel slavery was the first
time 'slavery acquired a color'. It was also the time in which whiteness
was created. Thus race can be viewed as a weapon created to justify
the trans-Atlantic slave trade. Since then, whiteness has become an ideal
which people are measured against. It has become the 'in group', thus
making anything that exists outside of this the 'out group'. Hundreds of
years later, within schools, the result of this is teachers feeling more of
an affinity towards students who look, act and speak like that standard.

---

## Reflection

1. What is your image of the ideal and successful student?
2. Who have been the most successful students in your experience?
3. What is their gender?
4. What racial and ethnic group do they belong to?
5. Working or middle class?

6. *Keep interrogating!*

7. Before we move on, take a minute to ask yourself: What does success for
   your students mean? How do we measure it? Is it measured by students'
   exam results, their wellbeing, their confidence in themselves? Who make the
   best leaders?
8. What are the traits of a good leader?

---

# What Is Bias?

There is a tendency to conflate being biased with having negative morals.
Academically speaking, bias is often referred to as a habit of the mind.
All biases are in fact a natural process and they are absolutely necessary
in conserving mental capacity. Humans, through an evolutionary process,
have developed the tools to use rational thought and not rely solely on
our instincts. Similarly, our physical responses to stimuli will be differentiated depending on the nature of the environment, stimulus, reflexes and
previous experiences. A slight rise in temperature may cause us to think

about removing an item of clothing, where touching a hot stove will elicit a reflex action. Our brains rely on roads often traversed, through the creation of associations and stereotypes.

> Many are grounded in the premises that stereotypes comprise invariant, homogenous, evaluative judgements of a given group (e.g. income, gender or ethnic group), and that stereotypes enable judgements of group members to be made quickly and with cognitive ease. (Campbell, 2015, p. 519)

As a young boy I was part of a small cubs group (a younger version of scouts). I'd like you to imagine a small Boy of Colour who is a round-faced version of me with a cute neckerchief. Just hold that image and any thoughts around that in your head for a minute. Before my first camping jamboree, me being me, I felt that I had to read a book about snakes because I had no idea that the county of Shropshire was not littered with venomous snakes but, hey, that is the innocence of youth. I vividly remember learning a rhyme about the difference between safe corn snakes and dangerous coral snakes: 'Red before black is safe for Jack. Red touching yellow will kill a fellow.'

Unaware that these snakes are native to North America, I thought this an important piece of information, and I remember thinking that I needed to hold this rhyme in the front of my mind. Not surprisingly and thankfully I never encountered a snake in those few days away. I am not sure what my friends would have thought of me trying to show off my new knowledge, or, and this is the most likely scenario, me running a mile and screaming in fear.

Our brains are not designed to reason and access the knowledge needed to assess the danger in times of immediate peril as their primary function is survival. The need for this bias simply exists as a response dependent on the need to act quickly. Equally in times when danger is not always imminent, there is a propensity to use those pathways to save cognitive resources.

Earlier I asked you to picture a round-faced version of me in a cute neckerchief as a cub scout. Which images came to mind? What colour was the neckerchief and shirt I was wearing? What was my stature? Was I short or tall, skinny or chubby?

Although these associations are natural, sometimes these associations may become distorted, negative and problematic; let me reiterate, these habits and biases do not make you or I a morally evil person, but we must endeavour to try to stop them influencing our actions if we want to claim to be fair. As educators the following may be very uncomfortable but I urge you to stay with me. Urge is the right word, because you're choosing to read this book and you have the choice to put it down, continue to read or to even burn it.

---

## Reflection

1.    What are your associations around your current students?
2.    Do these associations impact your day-to-day lives and the lives of others, especially in our classrooms?
3.    Do you think teachers really treat all their students the same and/or fairly?

---

Let us think through your personal experiences with gender. For the sake of this exercise, we will interrogate how society traditionally structures the gendering of children (I do recognise that multiple genders exist). From my position as a cis gendered male I have seen thousands of images and experienced a similar number of scenarios in which boys were playing sport, being rough and boisterous. What were your experiences of boys and girls throughout your lifetime? Use Table 2.2 to help you.

Now onto race. List five Black male characters from literature, television and film and then pick out common traits each character holds.

1.
2.
3.
4.
5.

In my work the common themes which emerge are baldness, attractiveness, muscles, hypermasculinity, the ability to fight and sometimes make people laugh. (The baldness is probably primed from the fact that I am standing in front of them and I have very little hair on the top of my head, but the others I cannot attest to owning.) I would recommend you do a similar activity with other protected characteristics and their intersections, starting with Women of Colour, as in my own experience Women of Colour are nearly invisible in our society. An example of this is the data presented in the *Guardian* last year (Adams, 2020) that universities in the UK employed just 25 Black women as professors.

**Table 2.2**    What are your experiences of boys and girls?

| Boys | Girls |
|------|-------|
| 1 | 1 |
| 2 | 2 |
| 3 | 3 |
| 4 | 4 |
| 5 | 5 |

If you have made it this far, well done; and I mean that. You've got through the step of starting to interrogate yourself. As educators we all have a choice in what we choose to perpetuate. It is worth noting that this is not the case with our students as they are recipients regardless of what they choose. Remember you have a choice to put this book down and to disengage with the possible distress caused by these conversations. However, generally People of Colour do not, and most importantly, nor do your Students of Colour.

---

## Reflection

These narratives in our lives form those well-trodden pathways, our go-to options and possible sources of bias.

1. Looking at your own career, what are the thoughts and experiences you've had around students in your classrooms?
2. Who was most and least successful?
3. Which characteristics did they hold?
4. Where did their success come from?
5. Was it solely through personal achievements or did their teachers have a role to play?
6. Where did these expectations and associations come from?

---

# Stereotypes

Stereotyping is the tendency to draw on overly simple, and oftentimes exaggerated, beliefs about groups to make judgements about individuals (Allport, 1954). Stereotyping groups of people comes from the same need to conserve cognitive energy; it is truly difficult to not rely on your past experiences when greeted with someone or something new. To get to know an individual, their personal ins and outs, their thoughts and views, takes time and energy, so the brain takes the shortcuts (associations). Let's now dispel some common misconceptions about stereotypes.

- 'Positive stereotypes are good.'
- 'Asian people are good at science and maths.'
- 'Black people are great runners.'

The problem with positive stereotyping is that although on the surface they may seem like a reward, or to go some way toward redressing the societal equilibrium, they are equally as damaging as negative stereotypes.

Stereotyping occurs when value is fixed for an 'unknown quantity' before rationally and cognitively estimating that quantity. As a practitioner

I remember being told by a new headteacher that I didn't want to go down a curriculum or teaching and learning career route. That I needed and wanted a pastoral role: 'You're great with the students, it'll suit you better.' People of Colour are often typecast as being pastoral experts; I was great with children and I still am, but apart from roles in leading behaviour my CV lacks experience and screams towards pedagogy, curriculum and data. My experience should have been part of the discussion around my career. But that would take work and time. Leaders are often most prone to using the shortcuts of bias because they are normally very time poor and as a result rely on the quickness of bias.

---

### Case Study: Positive Stereotypes

As a young student, I loved learning, I mean I *loved* learning. At school I absorbed everything that my teachers had to teach me. My A-Levels led to an undergraduate degree in physics. Now, I adore physics and mathematical sciences; for that I have to give credit to the teachers and school system which nurtured me into the field. A shout-out to my maths and science teachers but most of all thank you to my father.

However, since my youth I have been obsessed with books and I have spent countless hours reading and writing fiction as well as poetry. Scanning through my youth I cannot think of one instance when a teacher built me up or even encouraged me to write in the same way as I was constantly told that sciences would be a great career for me. How many Brown male students are told they can be great writers, love books and pursue their literary passions? I certainly was not. I was explicitly told that I'd be better served in concentrating on my 'natural' aptitude in the mathematical sciences.

How much potential is lost because of the way we stereotype young People of Colour? How often are white people stereotyped into certain subjects or roles? Has this ever happened to you growing up? Have we fallen into the same traps?

---

## Confirmation Bias

The confirmation bias serves to further entrench our biases. It is the tendency to seek out and perceive information which serves to confirm one's pre-existing beliefs and to ignore information which conflicts with those beliefs. As a teacher you must have an understanding of where your biases lie when it comes to race, and be aware that the confirmation bias will seek to reinforce those preconceived notions and emphasise them as the norm.

## What Is the Impact of Stereotyping Our Students?

The impact of stereotypes has dual effects on students; through the medium of their teachers and the Pygmalion effect, in which teacher expectations of their students has a direct impact on student outcomes and, more dangerously, on the student themselves through phenomena known as the stereotype threat.

## Impact on the Self

When students belong to a known group for which negative associations exist a process called the 'stereotype threat' can impair academic performance and intellectual engagement. This is due to students experiencing concerns around confirming negative stereotypes of their group (Johns et al., 2008; Steele and Aronson, 1995; Steele et al., 2002; Taylor and Walton, 2011). Common racial stereotypes may stunt academic outcomes by making life harder for some of the students in your classroom through a process in which self-protective actions follow the stimulus of fear and shame. This was shown by Steele and Aronson (1995) who gave a mix of university students an examination. They set up three different conditions where the test was described as a:

1. 'Diagnostic of intellectual ability'
2. 'Problem-solving task that was a non-diagnostic of ability'
3. 'Challenge'

The act of telling participants that the test was a measure of their intelligence was enough to negatively impact the performance of Black students. Within the non-diagnostic group who were undertaking a problem-solving task, the performance of Black students drastically improved, seeing their scores match those of their white peers.

Stereotypes can be complex and may be applied through various perspectives depending on various characteristics people possess. Shih et al. (1999) completed an intersectional analysis (including various characteristics) of gender and race in the stereotype threat. They looked at South East Asian women. People of South East Asian heritage are often seen as a 'model minority' or the 'good immigrant' in the UK. As a result, model minorities have positive stereotypes incorporated around their academic success; simultaneously, women will have to contend with negative stereotypes around their achievement in some subject areas – largely those that are quantitative – due to their gender (Aronson et al., 1998; Steele, 1997, in Shih et al., 1999).

The stereotype threat was subtly primed through the use of pretest questionnaires; Asian women had either their gender or their race 'activated', and an assessment followed this in a (traditionally male) quantitative subject area. Their conclusion showed both a 'stereotype threat' and 'boost' in the cohort of participants. The number of questions answered increased when the positive racial stereotype was activated (54%) and decreased with the gendered stereotype (43%).

Similar patterns were observed when looking at the correct answers and accuracy.

Walton and Cohen (2003), in their collation of 43 studies across age, gender and race, found that this boost (they refer to it as a 'stereotype lift') is also seen in white students when examined in the presence of Black peers. The negative academic stereotypes of others actually raised their performance, suggesting that the presence of minorities in the room was enough to activate the phenomenon, which further exacerbated the racial inequities in the classroom. An analysis of the post-test data collected by Shih and colleagues found that making candidates aware of their group characteristics (through stereotype activation) had no impact on their motivation, specifically no impact on:

1. The effort that they exhibited.
2. The number of questions for which participants reported guessing the answers.
3. Participants' liking of the test.
4. Their assessment of how well they did on the test.
5. Their assessment of the test's difficulty.
6. Their assessment of their mathematical skills.

Taken together, the literature suggests stereotype threat negatively affects both situational and chronic risks to individuals' self-concept. Students are oblivious to these effects and both the stereotype threat and boost are present regardless of personal beliefs. If it is known that a stereotype exists, it is likely to impact outcomes as both processes are unknowingly adopted. Although the source of the 'stereotype boost' was not investigated by Shih et al. or Steele and Aronson, it is fair to suggest that this leads to an increase in confidence and the belief that they can do well on the exam as the inverse was found by Chung et al. (2010).

Anxiety is at the source of the stereotype threat. There is a negative response induced from the fear that one's actions will confirm the beliefs of others and, more importantly, themselves (Aronson et al., 1998; Steele and Aronson, 1995). This means that telling Students of Colour to try harder, work harder, and put in more effort may be pointless. It will not alleviate the stereotype threat and likely will contribute to students' anxieties, exacerbating the whole issue. Whereas the stereotype boost bolsters a sense of pride, the stereotype threat arises out of a sense of shame.

You may be reading this and thinking that educators should capitalise on that pride and use positive stereotypes to the advantage of our students. However, this overt process may cause individuals to feel pressure to conform to the group's standard. This pressure in turn points to a fall in mental focus and concentration and led to participants in the aforementioned study being 'significantly impaired' in their mathematical performance. Where positive stereotypes are known to students, the stereotype boost may be likely to be observed; however, when an external audience expects a higher performance, these effects are moderated through students' fears around meeting those expectations, leading to a 'choking under pressure' (Cheryan and Bodenhausen, 2000).

In conclusion, if a student belongs to a racial group for which a known negative stereotype exists, or there is an expectancy of a positive stereotype, academic performance is likely to be hampered. These obstacles present both mentally and physiologically. Beasley and Fischer (2012) collated research in which the stereotype threat has been shown to reduce academic attainment through physiological stress response increases in blood pressure (Blascovich et al., 2001; Mendes and Jamieson, 2012), a reduction in working memory (Schmader and Johns, 2003) as well as protective disengagement from the task to save students' self-esteem (Aronson et al., 1998).

Let me reiterate.

The stereotype threat impacts the **physical** state of Students of Colour:

> First, the threat of confirming a negative stereotype induces uncertainty about one's performance: This activates a physiological stress response (e.g., increased blood pressure, cardiovascular threat reactivity, sympathetic nervous system arousal). (Schmader and Hall, 2014, p. 32)

Performance is hampered by the above process because, while a student is reconciling the stereotypes in their heads, they are using precious cognitive resources to remove those anxieties and worries which leads to mental fatigue (Schmader and Hall, 2014). While a student is subconsciously having to deal with those pressures, they are not using the same brain power as their white counterparts on the learning or assessments they are supposed to be doing.

## Psychological Management: Fighting the Impact of the Stereotype Threat

Teachers should aim to disrupt the stereotype threats from society in their students. This is based on their practice in psychological management as well as the learning environment, community and belonging. The shame of stereotypes comes from one of two sources, the shame of confirming a negative stereotype to oneself and to the white majority (Shapiro et al., 2013). So, the interventions fall under one of two umbrella headings: (a) letting yourself down, or (b) failing your group by conforming to negative stereotype.

## Self-integrity

Self-integrity is a measure of regarding yourself as being good, virtuous, and efficacious; being part of a valued (positively stereotyped) group is a major source of these things. White students generally have higher levels of 'self-integrity' than Students of Colour. This is because our world is framed toward whiteness; whiteness is the norm, it is everywhere, it is inherent in every facet of life. The process of the creation of a leadership prototype is a good example of normalisation. This process is where white people often see themselves reflected in leadership roles, giving them an idea of what they can aspire to.

Self-integrity is also increased by society's tendency to see whiteness as being virtuous (Feagin, 2010). When an abhorrent act occurs from a person from an 'out group', society is always quick to associate the act to that othered group. When an Islamist terrorist commits an atrocity there is commonly a call for leaders to justify their religious positions and the morality of their community; race and religion are questioned simultaneously. Think about a case of white supremacist or far-right extremist terrorism; actually can you think of any? Do you remember the family of the perpetrator being interviewed? Did you question the person's ethnicity? Did you start to feel a fear of all white people? How many of us would be able to acknowledge that this form of terrorism is the fastest growing threat in the UK and that more white people have been arrested over terrorism than any other racial group in 2018, 2019 and 2020 (Dearden, 2021; see also Allen and Kirk-Wade, 2020)? Do we as a society ever demand an explanation and justification from white community leaders? Do you see the difference?

A function of 'virtuous whiteness' means that we rarely interrogate the values and actions of white societies. White people rarely associate themselves with the negative aspects of their society (especially when talking about racism) and are allowed to use the 'few bad apples' ploy, a technique rarely afforded to People of Colour. White folx are afforded the virtues of their collective actions and are allowed to disregard the immorality of the individual communities. In our classrooms there is very little we can change about the standardised societal frame. However, there is work that could be applied to change the impact on those in the 'othered' groups. Having to feel like you will fall into the bracket of a negative stereotype takes its toll on your idea of self. It makes sense that bolstering self-integrity and worth provides a buffer to this form of the stereotype threat; it leads to greater motivation, sense of belonging and self-efficacy, all of which can snowball into a success avalanche.

## Bolstering Self-worth – Self-affirmation

Self-affirmation is a process where an important aspect of your life which is different from the stereotype threat (such as intelligence on an upcoming exam) is reflected on, emphasised and made salient (Sherman and Cohen, 2006). This reduces the stereotype threat in academic situations. Martens et al. (2006) found that women underperformed when told that the test they were set was a diagnostic of maths intelligence and a measure of their 'abilities and limitations', and elicited the stererotype threat. However, those who had undergone self-affirmation performed at a similar level to men and women who don't experience stereotype threat conditions.

Psychological interventions that increase the store of self-integrity are shown to decrease the impact of the stereotype threat and they lead to a remarkable impact on outcomes. This process provides a psychological buffer against effects of stereotype threat in schools, as this threat is reiterated throughout a student's life, and providing this buffering early on may lead to long-lasting benefits.

---

### ACTIVITY: Values Affirmation

Try this with your classes:

1.  Ask your students to choose their most important value from a list of values.
2.  Ask them to reflect on why they chose that value.
3.  Have them write a brief paragraph about why their chosen values were important to them.
4.  Finally, ask them to evaluate their level of agreement concerning their selected value.

(Sherman and Cohen, 2006)

---

Educational researchers investigated the above intervention, which lasted 20 minutes at the beginning of students' first term of the academic year. Students of Colour who completed the values affirmation intervention showed gains in all academic outcomes. These positive effects on the outcomes of Students of Colour were not only evident in the subject area in which the intervention was applied, but also the overall grades of all ability ranges. The lowest impact was seen for high-performing Students of Colour so this would suggest that these students already have higher levels of self-integrity and thus they are more adept at side-stepping the stereotype threat.

The bolstering of self-integrity through affirmation impacted positively on 70% of Students of Colour, reducing the racial achievement gap by 40% (Sherman and Cohen, 2006), in the addition of multiple affirming exercises (three to five times) in a school year. This presented as higher grades two years later, which were especially noticeable in the core subjects: science, maths, humanities and English (Cohen et al., 2009) even increasing the likelihood of Latinx and Black students' uptake at university (Goyer et al., 2017).

How did short 20-minute interventions have such a long-lasting impact? Psychological interventions are not the same as teaching curriculum content in that the time spent teaching does not always equate to outcomes. Let me invoke an analogy from biology, 'the law of minimum'. An organism's growth is dependent on multiple variables, stunting factors and resources. When a plant lacks magnesium, this impacts chlorophyll production and makes leaves turn yellow. It doesn't matter what other nutrients are available; growth is stunted as the leaves are damaged and this is the factor that holds the whole plant back. However, if we are able to introduce more magnesium into the soil, we have accelerated growth!

Having an increase in self-integrity means that you and your group have worth regardless of the result of this test; this alleviates the need to expel the anxiety caused by the stereotype threat. While self-affirmation may improve the outcomes of Black students, first-generation university students (Harackiewicz et al., 2014, in Hecht et al., 2019) and women (Miyake et al., 2010, in Hecht et al., 2019) from the stereotype threat, it did not have an adverse effect on white students (Cohen et al., 2009; Sherman and Cohen, 2006), males, or second generation university students (Martens et al., 2006). In adding psychological interventions with the aim to bolster self-integrity there is nothing to lose for any students.

## Conclusion

Biases are a natural part of our psyches; they are as normal as physical reflex actions. Trying to fight their existence through denial or avoidance serves no one. The first step in the classroom is a leap of faith to accept society's norms and then work to stop those seeping into our actions. Biases lead to stereotypes which have a two-fold impact, one centred on the student and the other on their teachers. Teachers who are secretly and unknowingly enamoured by the allure and ease of stereotypes may lower the expectations of groups of pupils, ultimately impacting on Brown and Black students' self-worth, and self-integrity which may lead to a negative self-fulfilling prophecy.

Those stereotypes will also have an impact on what Students of Colour think about themselves. Although these associations will still exist outside of the walls of your schools and organisations, within our walls we should endeavour to create a safe environment where young people can best prepare themselves for the society outside.

Those same stereotypes will also have an impact on the students they are directed towards, which they will have to contest with both inside and outside of your educational space. I believe that schools are like families. Like a family, they offer a safe space where children can learn and prepare themselves for life outside the sanctity of home walls. While we have little control over Students of Colour having their sense of self challenged in external spaces, it's our duty to embrace and celebrate them in our classrooms.

## Chapter Takeaways

- Interrogate your existing associations. Acknowledge and accept that they exist. This is not about malice, it's about humans being inculcated into collectives.
- Think about the acts you have committed and will commit through a racial lens.
- Biases and stereotypes will impact on perception.
- Consider how you have reinforced existing stereotypes about your students.
- Work to create environments where all students have a greater sense of self-concept and self-integrity through practices such as value affirmations.
- Actively try to ameliorate the racialised stereotype effect.

# How Our Racial Lens Perceives Behaviour

It is generally recognized today that no scientific definition of race is possible … Race would seem to be a dynamic and not a static conception, and the typical races are continually changing and developing, amalgamating and differentiating. (Du Bois, 1903)

## Introduction

When in the classroom, teachers are often asked to manage behaviour. I have issues with this 'managing' of behaviour, as the language suggests that educators are tasked with implementing actions that lead to controlled outcomes. Students are human beings, and controlling them is not only tricky but wrong. The best an educator can aim for is that we teach and support students in making better decisions. This choice of change is completed by teaching them to be better.

Behaviour in the classroom should be viewed as a teaching opportunity. If a child has difficulty reading or writing, we teach them and equip them with the tools to be better. This archaic idea that we punish people out of making bad choices is nonsense. There is rarely, if ever, a road to Damascus moment: 'I'm tired of being made to sit in silence. I am going to change the way I act.' If punitive systems worked, we would see immediate changes in behaviour, and the need for them wouldn't exist in schools or in adult life as prisons would be obsolete too.

One of the most important and effective tools we have in 'managing' behaviour is managing our own behaviour. There are invisible forces that impact our thoughts and, in turn, our own behaviour in the classroom. You'll notice that a lot of the studies and examples used in this chapter are based around Black children. Blackness is often linked with aggression and criminality; these stereotypes in our society are commonplace and actively leak into our actions. This chapter will not address behaviour management of the classroom. It will present the ways in which teacher bias influences teachers' and consequently students' behaviour and how this plays out in the classroom.

## Data

Part of my work revolves around the data created by the school's behaviour for learning culture. This is an indicative measure of teacher bias in behaviour records held in education establishments. Most schools keep records for extended periods, and there are rich stories hidden throughout them. Let's first address how perception influences our objectivity. As teachers, we all feel that we treat our students with a level of equality and that race doesn't ever figure in the equation, and I am now talking candidly; yet the chances are that race already acts as a large factor in all our decisions.

Racial bias infiltrates every element of our society. We know that our classrooms can contribute to the schools-to-prison trajectory for some pupils; as we explore the biases in both schools' behaviour and our country's judicial systems we find striking parallels. The fairest place in the land should be our law courts; after all, Justice does wear a blindfold. In the UK, sentences are handed out by the presiding judge, who is given a set of guidelines detailing possible sanctions. So, one would assume there would be no difference in sentencing between People of Colour and white people. However, the raw data throws up worrying trends. As you can see from Table 3.1 both male and female BAME groups are more likely to be sentenced to prison while being less likely to have previous cautions or convictions.

By evaluating the data further, Kathryn Hopkins et al. produced reports looking at the likelihood of imprisonment (as opposed to other punishments such as community sentence, suspended sentence order, or discharge) across several different variables (Hopkins, 2011; Hopkins et al., 2015). She uses a logistical regression; in layman's terms, this is a mathematical tool that provides an odds ratio, which shows many more times an occurrence is likely to happen (see Table 3.2).

**Table 3.1**    Logistic regression model for sentencing to prison decisions

| Group | Likelihood of offenders *not* having previous cautions or convictions | Likelihood to be sentenced to prison |
|---|---|---|
| BAME females | 53.2% | 11.4% |
| BAME males | 72.8% | 20.7% |
| White females | 73.8% | 7.6% |
| White males | 84.6% | 16.2% |

*Source*: Hopkins (2011). Republished with permission, under the Open Government Licence.

In 2011 you were almost 40% more likely to receive a prison sentence if you were from a BAME community than if you belonged to the white group, and 56% more likely if you were not a UK national. Remember, this

**Table 3.2**  Logistic regression model for the likelihood of being sentenced to prison, for those convicted and sentenced for indictable offences at the Crown Court 2011

| Factors | | Odds ratio |
|---|---|---|
| Demographics | (White) | 1.390*** |
| | BAME | |
| | (Female) | 1.825*** |
| | Male | |
| | Age at sentence | 0.997*** |
| | (Under 18 years old) | |
| | 18 to 21 | 4.059*** |
| | 22 to 25 | 4.510*** |
| | 26 to 30 | 4.684*** |
| | 31 to 40 | 4.245*** |
| | 41 to 50 | 3.523*** |
| | 51 and older | 3.502*** |
| | (UK national) | |
| | Non-UK national | 1.562*** |

*** denotes a statistical significance

( ) denotes the reference category

Source: Hopkins (2011). Republished with permission under the Open Government Licence.

is after you statistically remove the other variables. It seems that Justice is peeping through that piece of cloth. In today's progressive world, we would expect to be hurtling towards equality. Four years later, the data looks even worse. In 2015 the statistical analysis was more forensic and broken down into different racial groups. You are at least 50% more likely to receive a custodial sentence if you are of Colour than if you are white (see Table 3.3).

One of the starkest trends in the data fell in the drug band: committing a drug offence as a Person of Colour leaves you 236% more likely to be

**Table 3.3**  Logistic regression model for the likelihood of being sentenced to prison, for those convicted and sentenced for indictable offences at the Crown Court 2015

| Effect | Odds ratio |
|---|---|
| (White) | |
| Asian | 1.551*** |
| Black | 1.533*** |
| Chinese or other | 1.814*** |

*** denotes a statistical significance

( ) denotes the reference category

Source: Hopkins et al. (2016). Republished with permission under the Open Government Licence.

imprisoned when compared to a white person. It seems that Justice is not blindfolded, equality isn't her aim and she has a disliking for melanated people. If you are a Person of Colour you are more likely to go to jail for committing the same crimes as white folx. One can only assume that judges look at the infractions of those of us of Colour with more disdain. Stop, I am not calling any one person racist, I am also not saying this is a deliberate act. I do not believe this is down to overt racism. As People of Colour being disadvantaged exists here as a system-wide issue, it is likely the result of implicit process.

---

## Reflection

1.  If in a court of law bias is prevalent then what about in our schools? What about your context?
2.  Think through your experiences of punitive systems: who are the students who are targeted by the consequences?
3.  Could you hold an unconscious disdain for students of Colour when dealing with behaviour incidents? Reflect on your interactions.
4.  Are we equally as likely to observe infractions with white students?

---

## Perception of Behaviours

This may take some effort, but I ask you to humbly keep any defensive emotions in check. Your perceptions of students' behaviour are racially prejudiced. You have been taught this. In our biased society, we are taught to see Black people (and Blackness) as being associated with aggressive acts and aggression. This was shown clearly when white subjects were shown what they thought was a videotape of an ongoing interaction happening in another room – the tape showed an ambiguous act (a shove). The same action was perceived and labelled as more violent when committed by a Black man than when the push originates from white hands (Duncan, 1976).

The human brain can be split into discrete systems, comprised of an instant thinking process and a longer more inquisitive one. System 1 is described as being automatic; this system is instinctual. It is where bias lies completely subconsciously and thus acts quickly and with no or little effort. System 2 requires attention and effort that include more complex computations; it is a more rational part of the brain (Kahnemann, 2011). One simple way of looking at subconscious system bias is that your system 1 is as vulnerable as it has always been while system 2 rationalises your actions and brings forth the idea that you could possibly contribute to a racist society. That being said, system 2 should not be seen as a panacea. Yes, while thinking through and interrogating our actions we may be able to subvert some of the issues, but we have to also accept that we are taught to uphold white supremacist structures in everything that we do, including within our deeper rational thought.

---

## Reflection

1.  What impact does the perception of aggression have in addressing behavioural issues in the classroom?
2.  How does this correlate to disproportionate exclusions of Black students in UK schools?

---

Studies have shown that there is an expectancy to see rage in the actions of melanated people. In Hugenberg and Bodenhausen's (2003) study, participants were found to have greater readiness to see Black faces as angry when compared to white faces, albeit through an implicit process. Even in the school setting, both Black and white children rated behaviours as being 'meaner' and more threatening when the perpetrator was Black rather than when they presented as white (Sagar and Schofield, 1980). Neutral Black children's faces are perceived as being more threatening than those of their white counterparts by teachers (Halberstadt et al., 2018). Black faces are even easier to remember when associated with anger (Ackerman et al., 2006). Here we have multiple consequences in the school setting, starting with expectations impacting the pupils' self-worth, perceptions of students, their testimony and the inherent sense of fear that Black students may bring.

Racial stereotypes may also induce this sense of fear. When presented with Black faces there was an improvement in the reaction time in recognising weapons and the data seems to suggest that this process is automatic (Payne, 2001). This work was built on by Eberhardt et al. (2004), in which the seeing of Black faces for milliseconds leads to an improvement in recognition of degraded images associated with crime (knives and guns). The association of crime and Blackness was clearly demonstrated. This anxiety induces white participants' strong tendency to see anger but no other emotions in neutral Black faces (Cottrell and Neuberg, 2005; Maner et al., 2005). Devine (1989) showed both high and low prejudiced people made more stereotypical observations (when unconsciously primed), evaluating a paragraph about a person showing ambiguously hostile behaviour. They found that candidates perceived that the actor was being more hostile when presented as Black. If our basic instinct is that Black students are to be viewed as threatening and feared, the next step is to protect ourselves and others. So, I ask is it any wonder that Black students are disproportionately excluded from schools in the UK?

## Recording Behaviour (Words not Tone)

Working within educational organisations, behaviour records form an integral part of the picture of the school's culture. First, when analysing behaviour records, remember that they are not a record of the interaction that happened, but they are a record of the teacher's perceptions of what happened. If we start from the position that all behaviour including both reward and sanctions should be spread evenly without racial prejudice, we then start to find useful trends. In my experience Black students are most likely to receive a sanction for defiance or, traditionally speaking, 'talking back'. How do you remove the teachers' bias from the records? As I noted previously, the brain can be split into the instinctive and the rational systems. The instinctive system 1 will use associations and react on the spot if we do not use inhibitive voluntary structures from system 2 and this is problematic. Consciously calling upon and using system 2 is how we begin to ameliorate the impact of the damage once the interaction has happened.

Digging further into the records we often find the descriptions of the misdemeanours concerning Students of Colour to be more emotive in nature than those of white students. This is because our memories, once the events have occurred, are often tainted with bias. The use of system 1 is automatic but only by constantly questioning its validity, through using system 2 (the more rational part of the brain) to justify those original perceptions, do we start to undo the damage wrought.

A simple but effective method is using 'words not tone'. When completing behaviour logs the only thing staff may write are the words that are used by all parties involved; reports of the posture, tone and other factors are so prone to bias that they colour everything. Being forced to remember and record the words spoken activates system 2's evaluative functions and this is where we start to break down any possible biases. This process has the advantages of fewer sanctions being recorded overall due to the knock-on effect of providing the impetus for teachers to evaluate interactions as they happen.

---

### Case Study: Recording Behaviour

John entered the room approximately 2 minutes late. The students aggressively moved through the classroom with their jackets on and refused to engage when challenged politely about uniform. They pushed their chairs back forcefully and took an inordinate amount of time in getting their books ready for work. When using terms like 'aggressive', 'polite', 'forcefully', and 'inordinate amount' of anything, do we ever consider the bias behind them? How

*(Continued)*

> many times will white pupils who behave in exactly the same way never be described in that manner? Is that because their behaviour felt different? That you didn't even notice? Or that we give them a bit of leeway because they look like you or fit the norm?

You may be reading this thinking you're not like that, these biases live in other people, they do not inhabit your classroom or school. Well I would urge you to reconsider the method that brought you to this conclusion. We should attempt to divorce ourselves from our perception and the 'objective' reality. When we look at the perception of and commentary on behaviour events, we find that when communicating an aggressive interaction between a white aggressor wielding a deadly razor, 50% of participants moved that razor into Black hands after a chain of communication (Allport, 1954). Boon and Davis (1987) carried out a similar study in the UK and they solely measured the recall value using a forced option choice and longer description tasks. They found evidence of the commitment effect, that is, having once chosen an answer, the brain contorts memory towards that commitment. Participants either had to decide immediately who had the knife (forced option choice) and then write the description, or vice versa. Participants writing the description before deciding who held the knife gave more accurate results of the knife being held by the white person. Those who had to decide immediately 'saw' the knife in the hands of the Black person.

## Special Educational Needs: Social and Emotional Mental Health Needs (SEMH)

When compared to white youth, some ethnic and racial minority youth are more likely to receive a diagnosis of disruptive behaviour disorders and are less likely to receive a diagnosis of ADHD. When controlling for confounding variables such as adverse childhood experiences, prior juvenile offences, genetics, and socio-demographics, these diagnostic and treatment disparities remain (Morgan et al., 2013 and Coker et al., 2016).

Professor Steven Strand from the University of Oxford identifies that extensive research found that Black Caribbean British students are substantially more likely to be identified with Special Educational Needs than any other ethnic and racial group (Strand and Lindorff, 2018). Using England's national pupil database, which uses data from over 6 million students, the study was conducted over 10 years and found that Black Caribbean British students were 2.24 times more likely to be assessed as having social, emotional and mental health issues. Logistical regression was used here; by allowing the study to remove the social economic factors (measured through free school meals and student postcodes) the odds ratio falls to 1.43, but there is no reason for this number to be this high. This is particularly problematic because the label of SEMH may lead to lower expectations, aspirations and a change in curriculum, and sometimes even a movement into a new provision. Strand concluded:

> From the factors that we have measured – socio-economic background, poverty and neighbourhood deprivation, and children's development on entry to school – we can't explain why, in particular, Black Caribbean children and mixed-Black-Caribbean-and-white children are more likely to be diagnosed with SEMH. (Professor Steven Strand, in Richardson, 2019)

These assessments are often based on a deficit model; educational psychologists often work on the premise that there is no smoke without fire when arriving at a consultation. The problem seems to be multifaceted in the referral of the child for assessment as well as the process itself. With the number of SEMH assessments (formerly known as BESD, or behaviour, emotional, social disorders) there has been no decrease in the number of referrals since the change of the label, so it can be inferred that behaviour plays a primary role in referrals. It is worth pointing out that these assessments are based on an observation of behaviour or, should I say, a perception of behaviour. Any assessments of behaviour should recognise the nature of the teacher's, psychologist's and student's positionality and centre on the student's experiences. Simply, all behaviour is difficult to assess because it is not objective, but highly subjective.

> Is it that these young people from this ethnic group are more confrontational with their teachers because of gang culture or is it a perception of their behaviour? (Professor Steven Strand, in Richardson, 2019)

## Our Everyday Culture

Weisbuch et al. (2009) investigated the link between body language and nuances in facial expression in popular TV shows and implicit associations of those who watch them. They found that both verbal and nonverbal communication caused an increase in unconscious racial bias in viewers. Through the ideomotor principle this activation is said to move from memory of representations of the acts perceived to unconsciously held preconceptions (Berkowitz, 1984). They looked at 11 popular shows, removed audio, and cropped the subject out of the scene to show only the other characters. White participants were then asked if the missing person in the clip was being treated positively and whether they were liked by the visible characters on a scale from +3 to –3. They found a significant positive bias towards white characters; only in 18% of clips observed were Black characters viewed as having a slightly more favourable non-verbal response from other characters. Crucially, white participants were unable to spot a non-verbal race bias pattern when present; this means there is an exertion of non-conscious influence. When the white judges were presented with the transcript of the clips (without being told the race of the characters), the results showed that both white and Black characters did not actually differ in their elicitation of favourable responses.

These messages constantly bombard our psyches. Simultaneously, we are taught not to judge books by their covers, propagating the very 'British' value of tolerance and conscious acceptance of equality. This leads to a reinforcement of the nature of the prejudice, which is subtle and modern; hence many people are reluctant to accept its existence at all (Bargh and Chartrand, 1999).

## Reflection

1.  In schools, what does the impact of non-verbal and non-conscious implicit bias lead to?
2.  Which students do we hold with positive regard and what are their common traits?
3.  Now, if you are brave enough, do the same with the students you don't hold with positive regard.

# What Can We Do as Educators?

## Imitation

As educators one of the best tools in any classroom situation is our own behaviour. Rather than second-guessing and making assumptions about the children in our classrooms, whether that's conscious or not, we need to interrogate bias's impact on our thoughts, behaviour, and how we treat students in our classroom.

Let us start with the problematic psychological consequence of the 'imitate effect'. Humans imitate from the moment we are born. Toddlers mouth words that their carers use around them and mimic the mannerisms of their favourite television programmes. Where does this need to 'copy' originate? Some psychologists believe that it is prewired at birth; others, who are proponents of the associative learning model, suggest this is how schemata are structured and that imitation forms a vital part of learning.

Whatever the origin of this effect, mimicking is both unconscious and automatic. Have you ever found yourself tapping your foot in the same way as someone close by or picking up parts of an accent or dialect in your speech? Many educators will (consciously and unconsciously) mirror their students' behaviours to build rapport and connect with them when they are in a state of distress.

One of my father's favourite phrases is 'smile, and the whole world smiles with you'. This has some real truth within it. We move our faces unconsciously in all interactions as it is an integral part of connecting. Subtle mimicry in our facial features plays a vital role in communication and how our brain acknowledges the nature of the interaction at hand. So much so that when the ability to imitate facial nuances is inhibited by asking people to chew gum, it becomes harder to recall the faces of people we meet (Zajonc et al., 1982).

## Leakage

Once stereotype activation has occurred, a process of 'leakage' impacts the teacher's behaviour. For example, an educator sees an altercation in the playground between a Black pupil and a white pupil. When addressing the Black pupil, teachers may posture differently, subtly change their tone, furrow their brow, use a different dialect, raise or lower their voice, or any number of gestures. Through a process of imitation, the pupil then may respond in kind. Both parties are unaware of their actions at this point as their communication has been impacted through an automatic process, meaning their responses are entirely unconscious.

## The Crux Point

In the previous chapter, we discussed stereotypes. Stereotypes can be activated by various observations: skin colour, hair texture, and so on. These stereotypes, such as Black males being aggressive, are activated automatically without the teacher's conscious recognition. Stereotype activation can set behaviours into motion without teachers being aware that triggers even existed; this can make identifying the source near impossible. In the school scenario, after a stereotype has been activated, the teacher's behaviour often dictates the consequence of any further interaction. Does the teacher stop and defuse the situation? Do they recognise that their student may not be adept at self-regulating? Is there some conscious recognition that their actions may have provided the spark for this educational tinder box? Unfortunately, this reflection is often overridden by the need to react to the apparent disdain reaction through the student's facial

**Table 3.4**  A possible interaction between student and teacher denoting conscious and subconscious thought processes

| Interaction | Response | Thoughts |
| --- | --- | --- |
| Students in an altercation | Conscious: Teacher moves to split up the altercation. | What is going on here? |
| Black pupil engages in dialogue | Unconscious: Stereotype is activated through a racial marker. | Why is this child constantly causing trouble? |
| Teacher's stereotype leaks into communication | Unconscious: Teacher's facial expressions, tone and volume of voice subtly conveys the stereotypical response. | The teacher is completely unaware. |
| Pupil responds through imitation | Unconscious: Student mirrors teacher's expressions. | The pupil is completely unaware. |
| Teacher reacts to signs of aggression in students and acts | Conscious: Teacher acts on the information they now observe. | Why is this child acting like this? I knew it would be this way. |

*Source:* Adapted from Earp (2010)

expression (tone, volume, posture, etc.). The association emphasises the student's negative actions, which reinforces the original, long-standing stereotype, and the cycle forever continues.

Consequently, the pupil is now in danger of being put into a self-fulfilling prophecy because of how the teacher's brain has automatically categorised their behaviour; see examples in Table 3.4.

Our students learn to adapt to our reactions to survive that interaction. As a Person of Colour, I am very aware of this effect, so I have had to change my behaviour to survive in different scenarios. Boys of Colour are taught or learn very quickly that keeping silent, nodding your head, softening your voice, wearing clothes that are deemed safe and keeping your face as neutral as possible is always advisable, regardless of whether they are a good person. You learn that you can rarely win in our world and realise that right and wrong mean very little in many situations.

Although I have accented the educator's role, all school interactions are two-way; teachers are not the only people involved in these interactions. Students are likely to come into your classrooms with similar preconceived notions and thoughts that may trigger unconscious processes and then conscious actions. This is not a matter of fault, but the aim is to disrupt these cycles for everyone's betterment.

We have all met the students who come with a tough outer exterior. These students may have had to present this façade as they navigate society where a completely different set of rules are at play for them

(Anderson, 1999; Stewart et al., 2006). Remember Students of Colour will arrive at school with multiple experiences of racism. We often forget that all discrimination is a form of violence that has a traumatic impact. Many children exposed to violence will present with stress, irritability and hypervigilance (Gorman-Smith and Tolan, 1998). Educators must aim to keep all of that in mind, and their own emotions in check, before unconsciously parroting their students' actions.

## How Do We Stop the Cycle?

### 'Don't think about pink elephants'

What are you thinking about?

The command in the latter part of the sentence is the part that sticks. It's challenging to stop that mental process of thinking about those pink elephants. There are techniques to veto those actions. Distraction is one successful method, where you consciously force your brain to think of something else. Have a go. Force yourself to concentrate on something other than those elephants.

Obviously, this distraction technique becomes more difficult when under stress and exhaustion. You are more likely to fall in to biases in your action when you are rushed and tired. These distractions will move the mind, which in turn will ameliorate the bias in your actions. The idea that perception is the source of our actions is over a century old. William James in 1890 detailed the 'ideomotor theory of action' which speaks to body movements that arise in observers watching other people performing certain actions (Knuf et al., 2001, p. 779). The theory suggests that every mental representation of a movement awakens to some degree the actual action. Thus, the ideomotor theory leads to the premise that observing, thinking about or imagining a behaviour can increase the likelihood of it presenting (Knuf et al., 2001).

The research cited above concentrates on the direction from activation to action, but James's ideomotor approach does not deny or preclude the reverse. Physical activities may induce internal images. In the above example, if there is a set routine of mental representations triggered unknowingly by the pupil's traits, the teacher's consequent actions to alleviate racial bias may change the cognitive processes at the heart of the issue. In a school setting it is useful to pause and deliberately go through the steps of an internal script, which has the added benefit of questioning the bias process as it happens. It is something we can all fall back on when tired and rushed.

## Script

1.  What do I expect is going to happen next?
2.  How am I evaluating the interaction?
3.  What feelings did I have the last time this happened?
4.  How did I react the last time this happened?

    And then:

5.  What does the student expect to happen next?
6.  What feelings does the student have about these interactions?
7.  How are they likely to feel and react given their experience?

If we follow a course multiple times, those journeys also become the well-trodden pathways regardless of whether it leads to a pot of gold. Psychologists have found empirical evidence (Mischel and Shoda, 1995; Shoda et al., 1994) that all responses can become automatic if they are repeated enough times. This is why the reinforcement of the original stereotype of 'I knew this pupil would act like that' is problematic. The more automated your tendency towards your bias, the more difficult it is to acknowledge and unpick.

The automaticity is a severe problem, but at the same time there is a hidden gem, no, a piece of coal waiting to be pressurised into a diamond. If we forge our consciousness into the processes of interrupting our actions, this too, in time, may become automatic.

---

## Reflection

1.  Think of a time when you had to manage conflict between two students from different racial/ethnic backgrounds. Think about the children. Did they bring any biases to their exposition? How was the dissonance resolved?
2.  Now think about yourself. Did you bring any biases to the table? What was the resolution? Was it free of those associations? What would you have done differently?

---

# Ethnocentric Behavioural Culture

Eye contact in my and many cultures is something that is accepted once a level of respect has been earned as is the language we use. For example, when I was about 16 my father for the first time started referring to me as Pranav bhai (brother); this is like a rite of passage, from child to adult. Why do those and similar cultural standards mean less in our classrooms than those upheld through whiteness?

---

### Case Study: Cultural Differences

As a primary school child, I remember being sent out of the classroom, standing outside the door and contemplating what was about to come. The corridor is long and lonely, and while reflecting on my actions, I felt a deep sense of shame. Thinking back now to my posture, my shoulders are rounded, my back hunched, and my head hangs low. I am sullen. To find some comfort, I remember slowly but surely leaning back towards the wall next to my classroom door … As soon as my back touched the wall, a teacher towers over my small frame, made smaller by my need to cover the guilt, and says firmly, 'I can't believe how disrespectful this is. First you have been disruptive in the classroom and now you can't even stand up straight.' This memory, although faded into sepia, is now vividly dancing around my body; standing up tall felt wrong, and it took an effort to do so. Then came something that changed my relationship with school and society for ever.

The simple phrase: 'look me in the eye.'

For many of you, this may seem absurd, but remember, being British does not mean being white or having the white majority's culture. In many cultures, when committing an act of masti (mischief), the correct thing to do is drop your head deep and stare in silent contemplation at the ground and look appropriately admonished. Now from an adult in power I was told the complete opposite message.

The act of 'standing up straight' felt disrespectful; it felt like I was signifying that I was on equal standing with my teacher when I was wrong and felt terrible about what I had done. The request to look at an elder 'in the eye' blew my mind apart. This would be seen as an act of defiance at home. The act was like looking directly at a solar eclipse, forcing your gaze into position but knowing from the start it's incorrect and that hurt will follow.

---

I still have questions around the point of these fixed standards. Why would you seek to make eye contact with an adult, especially when you were being put right? When in the wrong, you'd never aim to double down but to accept and make amends. Respect is a given in my own household. I would never need to show adults that I respect them by engaging in ritualistic eye contact and standing bolt upright. Without the need to 'show respect' why would you seek to address a person in authority when you are being admonished?

This dissonance has a more profound impact than just causing trouble in the interactions with teachers; it teaches you that your culture is not accepted in this space because it is incorrect and inferior. As a child, you learn very quickly that there are two ways of being, and you cannot be successful while holding onto your identity, culture, birthright and personal safety in schools and then later, as a consequence, society.

For Students of Colour there is a need to alienate themselves from their culture in order to fit into the school culture, forcing them to maintain a difficult psychological balance between home and away, which can lead to a feeling of belonging to neither. This leads to a double consciousness, an internal conflict that affects the 'othered'. W. E. B. Du Bois, in his auto-ethnographical work *The Souls of Black Folk* (1903), describes this as a psychological challenge in which Black folk are always looking at 'one's self through the eyes' of whiteness. These are two examples of cultural dissonance that Students of Colour may have to navigate. It leads to education for Children of Colour often being a schizoid process.

---

## Reflection

1. Take a minute to reflect on the cognitive effort needed by Students of Colour to just exist in our society.
2. What space does that leave for learning and growing into an individual member of society?

---

> It is little wonder that the Black student rebels against this neurotic process which demands that he become not-self and shed his identity in order to succeed. (Wilson, 1978, p. 234)

Before we get too excited and start to rewrite behaviour for learning policies to include those seemingly dichotomous cultural standards, we must not make broad sweeping assumptions either. Do all BAME children have the same cultural norms? No. The world is a vast area filled with more than 7 billion people. To further put this into context, my father hails from an Indian state comprised of over 60 million people (this is similar to the total UK population). To assume that all of these people have the same cultural norms is illogical. That's before we even begin to account for the impact of being raised in a worldwide diaspora. We should teach students to navigate the UK's norms but this should not be to the detriment of their culture and/or their identity. We should seek to learn and build a sense of belonging over inclusion in our schools.

The current system encourages inclusion on its terms. How many of you reading this would suspect that my name is not Pran Patel? I'm not even Pranav; my is name is प्रणव My fui, that's father's sister, on the chhatti divas, named me under the rashi of Kanya; the name given to me, on the day that Hindus believe that I am written into the book of life, sounds nothing like the name I am referred to as. I learned from being in the school environment that it is simpler, no, necessary to anglicise my name, as my teachers and peers would not endeavour to learn to say my actual name. This culture does not create belonging; this is 'inclusion' under strict terms and conditions. It is essential to recognise there is no real choice here as it is enforced under duress.

If I were to come to your house to enjoy your hospitality and share a meal, I am sure you would greet me kindly at the door, show me the amenities, sit me down to eat, and tell me to make myself at home. Yes, I may feel included. For schools to serve all our students, the aim for inclusion should not be a panacea for all ills. In my guest appearance at your place, we have to remember that although I may feel welcome, I am, you are, and everyone else is aware this is not my home. The rules and etiquette are still yours to make, which is fine in this invitation to break bread together. However, schools are different places because they are not the sum of the buildings or leaders; in essence, schools are places where multiple people from many backgrounds form a community. Communities are not owned by the powerful but are where people build a shared sense of belonging through a joint culture.

## Treating Students the Same

Most behaviour for learning systems is based on the foundation that students are all treated the same, or in a similar fashion. All educators know that students are not exact and perfect machines, and as a result they, like us, react differently to stimuli in their environments and so context is always important. Now I'd like us to think about the way society treats Students of Colour. Do we as educators really understand what it is like for a Child of Colour navigating a world today?

In my own experience, I have been repeatedly:

- followed around shops by adults
- accosted by police
- dragged out of a car
- told that 'Darkies' (and other labels that I don't care to repeat) commit crimes
- spat at (and worse) in the street in broad daylight
- been told it's a shame I'm not white.

I could go on for pages. If we agree that context is important, do we ever consider the daily experience and, even more importantly, do we ever ask students about their current circumstances? Have we ever given them the space to discuss their feelings around this? Merton wrote in his essay (1948) that the 'self-fulfilling prophecy' has multiple effects on the perception of 'out groups', including the dichotic nature of observing and then categorising behaviours. Similar behaviour is evaluated differently depending on the person who is exhibiting it; white virtues are turned into Black and Brown vices. He asks what are the differences in the terms 'firm', 'obstinate' and 'pig headed'? The connotations are very different although in practice the outward appearance is exactly the same. What are the changes in behaviour by which you would differentiate people with those labels? Who are you more likely to attribute the more negative label to?

The most prevalent examples that Merton details are around aggression and anger. 'You're being aggressive.' Every Man of Colour I have ever interacted with has experienced this. Every one of us has seen a white counterpart described as passionate for the same behaviour. Similarly, Women of Colour are described as loud, sassy and angry, where white women are outspoken and ardent (Kendall, 2021; Saad, 2020).

Virtues for white folx are always virtues because this is what is expected of them. The same virtues may even be celebrated for a time when exhibited by People of Colour until one is seen to step out of their lane into the social strata of the 'in group'. This is the status quo and presents the 'in group' as propagating racism and protecting itself. I know of a school in London with a senior leadership team made up solely of Women of Colour who were accused of 'empire building' and discrimination by their local authority. Yet, in a city which is over 55% BAME an all white team is seen as common and the norm. White students who speak up and out are often seen as leaders while Students of Colour are trouble makers for the same actions. When we see groups of Black boys acting 'boisterous', would we have the same response as we would if we replaced those same students with a set of white girls?

## Case Study: Adultification by Youlande Harrowell

Every child deserves a childhood. Young People of Colour are often denied this right through a process of adultification.

The word 'innocence' is synonymous with childhood. However, for Black girls, this sentiment is rarely applied. A ground-breaking study in 2017 by the Georgetown Law's Center on Poverty and Inequality found that 'adults believe Black girls need less nurturing, less protection, less support and less comforting' (Blake and Epstein, 2019; Casas, 2017). This was supported by studies which have shown that Black girls are:

- 2.7 times more likely to be referred to the juvenile justice system
- 2 times more likely to be disciplined for minor violations like cell phone use
- 20% more likely to be charged with a crime.

These findings support the existence of the adultification bias faced by Black girls, who are disproportionately held to higher, and at times more 'adult'

*(Continued)*

standards than their white counterparts in the United States. These experiences are not isolated to the US.

Sadly, they reflect the lived experience of Black girls in the UK, whose childhood transgressions are perceived as intentional and malicious instead of immature decision-making. This is further complicated by the long-standing stereotypes of being loud, aggressive and angry, whereas white counterparts are characterised as boisterous, direct and frustrated.

The long-term impact of these views of Black girls have far-reaching ramifications. For example, if the view is held that Black girls need less nurturing and support, this 'may translate into fewer leadership and mentorship opportunities in schools' (Epstein et al., 2017).

In the UK, the discourse around unconscious bias continues to permeate our society. As a nation we are trying to navigate the stark lack of equity within our community. The adultification of Black girls is a strand in a thick bow of bias that plagues us. As always, what actions can be taken to prevent this bias from disadvantaging Black girls?

1. Reflect: Analyse your school's behaviour data. Who is being sanctioned? What behaviours are they being sanctioned for? What patterns are emerging? Which students are allowed to be treated like children?
2. Converse: Speak to your students and staff. How do they feel about the nature of sanctions being handed out? What feedback do they have about the experiences of different groups in your school's community?
3. Change: Based on the reflections and conversations had, what changes are needed to ensure parity, support and protection of your whole school community?

If research published over four years ago has not effected change, than what was the point? Let's face up to reality and start meaningful actions to ensure long-lasting change.
#LetBlackGirlsBeGirls

## Conclusion

As educators we need to recognise that young Black people are misdiagnosed as having more severe behavioural problems at higher rates than their white peers (Fadus et al., 2020; Strand and Lindorff, 2018). When danger presents in any context, including our schools, the human brain creates functions to protect itself from the anxiety. For Students of Colour vigilance can provide an important role in forming barriers to attacks on one's mental and physical wellbeing. The cost of this constant heightened state of hypervigilance impacts physiologically and psychologically through issues with sleep, the immune system and other health concerns (Clark et al., 2006; Hicken et al., 2013; Williams and Mohammed, 2009). All of which increases stress vulnerability and risk of negative health outcomes (Himmelstein et al., 2015).

I am saying that racial bias, subconscious bias, impacts the physical and mental health of Students of Colour. As an educator you have the ability to ameliorate the impact on the young people in your care. This has to be a conscious move against everything we were and are taught. There are no shortcuts here: every time we encounter and interact with our students what is the baggage we place on them and how do they suffer as a result?

## Chapter Takeaways

- Acknowledge that bias impacts your perception of behaviour.
- Use words not tone in recording and passing on incidents of behaviour.
- Question your previous experiences and your evaluation of the interaction and use an internal script to position yourself in a more neutral place.
- Include equity as opposed to equality into your practice.
- Question your virtues and vices ascription of students in your care.
- Start building a culture where behaviour is seen as relative to the people you serve.

## 4.

# Assessment and Systemic Discrimination

If one is lucky, a solitary fantasy can totally transform one million realities.
(Maya Angelou, *The Heart of a Woman,* 1981)

## Introduction

The need for assessment is based on the basic idea that educators, leaders and students need to know what has been learned and retained. One of the functions of assessment is that it can influence the next steps for the learner, the class and the actions of the teacher. What if I told you that most methods of assessment are prone to racial bias?

On the face of it, assessment could be viewed as objective. If a student gets the right answer then it's correct. Wrong. Assessment systems are not only prone to bias but also often predicated on white supremacist structures. Assessment is obviously closely linked to what we think of our students' ability and potential, and thus informs teacher expectations, which is critical to student outcomes. These expectations and thus outcomes also have a less obvious impact in today's classrooms on behaviour and pupil self-worth.

## A Brief Look at the IQ Test

The first time we encounter assessment by today's standards is the introduction of the Intelligence Quotient (IQ) test. Frenchman Alfred Binet initially developed this test, and it was later adapted by US psychologist Henry Herman Goddard in 1908 and then later by Lewis Terman in 1916. Terman and Goddard sought a test which measured 'innate abilities' and the 'theoretical maximum' intelligence was an assessment against a pre-defined specification. As you can imagine, from that day IQ tests have been used by those seeking to maintain the societal status quo. Goddard himself later promulgated the idea that the descendants of marriage produced 'normal functioning people' and those outside of marriage sired criminals and 'inferior people' (Benjamin, 2009).

As a worldwide recognised measure of intelligence, IQ has influenced several assessment systems. Before we look at the ins and outs of the system let us establish why IQ as a metric is problematic. While IQ claims to measure innate intelligence, there is a rise of 3 points on average per decade (the Flynn effect); this obviously is too large a rise to be explained by evolutionary science. So, the answer must lie in society moving towards an education which prepares people for this style of testing. The way people look at and process the world, and the way their brains are structured is impacted on by the culture in which they grew up. Fasfous et al. (2013), from the University of Granada, investigated Moroccan immigrants to Spain and a group of 'native' Spaniards. Researchers accounted for language (through non-verbal testing), socio-economic factors, education level, age and sex in their sample. They found that the immigrant groups were more likely to depend on different neuropsychological components (working memory, shifting attention and decision-making) from the 'native' Spanish group (who depended more on motor coordination and verbal memory) in their overall score.

Different cultures will have various factors which build upon cognitive functions, neural functions and neuronal structure (Fasfous et al., 2013). A person's culture impacts on the way their brain processes information and, even in this cohort where education and monthly income were similar and considering this as a measure of homogeneity, the Moroccan participants and their culture were assessed to be lower.

Is it that cultures from the Global South are inferior to Eurocentric cultures? Absolutely not. I don't believe this and nor should you. IQ tests do not measure intelligence but rather a form of intelligence which is linked to proximity to the dominant white culture. As Fasfous et al.'s study suggests, IQ tests measure an intelligence based on and designed within a particular Eurocentric system. This leads to the assertion that having ethnocentric neural traits means that you score higher on IQ tests, and you are then seen as more intelligent and subsequently more successful. If this is the basis of our measurement of intelligence, then the whole education system is inclined towards whiteness and white supremacy and everything that flows from it is the fruit of the poisonous tree.

## Reflection

1. Ask yourself, is our whole education system flawed and biased towards a white European culture?
2. What are the consequences of this?

# Teacher Expectations

Teacher expectations matter. Expectations don't just set the learning environment but directly impact on all classroom outcomes. Simply expecting your students to act or achieve increases the likelihood of that happening. The Pygmalion/Rosenthal effect is testament to the importance of those words. Rosenthal and Jacobson in 1968 published *Pygmalion in the Classroom* which originally proposed the idea that students' outcomes are impacted by their teachers' expectations of them.

Students in a Californian elementary school (equivalent to UK primary schools) were given a test to form a research baseline. Teachers were not made privy to individual outcomes but were later told that a random 20% (one in five) heralded results which indicated that these students would be 'intellectual bloomers'. The impact of telling teachers the names of that fifth led to the statistically significant improvements in those defined as 'intellectual bloomers' when students were retested a year later (Rosenthal and Jacobson, 1968).

> When we expect certain behaviours of others, we are likely to act in ways that make the expected behaviour more likely to occur. (Rosenthal and Babad, 1985)

Earlier, in Chapter 2 on teacher bias, we discussed the dangers of associations and the damaging impact this can have on Students of Colour. Teachers' perceptions and associations raise or lower their expectations of their students, which means this will ultimately affect students' outcomes. If a teacher (either consciously or unconsciously) believes that their Students of Colour will not achieve, this not only leads to direct damage but a continual loop of impact. These concepts are not particularly controversial as they are well-versed and widely accepted by most educationalists; the Rosenthal effect is cited tens of thousands of times. It is also evident in the UK Teachers' Standards, which are the minimum levels of practice expected from the viewpoint of being awarded qualified teacher status.

A teacher must:

1. Set high expectations which inspire, motivate and challenge pupils

   - Establish a safe and stimulating environment for pupils, rooted in mutual respect

   - Set goals that stretch and challenge pupils of all backgrounds, abilities and dispositions

   - Demonstrate consistently the positive values and behaviour which are expected of pupils.

## The Students Know What You Really Think about Them

We may not be verbalising the words explicitly but our students know what we really think about and expect of them. Babad, Bernieri and Rosenthal (1989) showed that adults (advanced education students) could spot differential teacher behaviours between students who they have low and high expectations of using audio-only and video-only taped footage. Interestingly, the most substantial effects were found for non-verbal teacher behaviours in the video-only tapes. We give ourselves away. These moderate biases lead to personal interactions which convey anxiety and discomfort, through non-verbal indicators such as distance, posture and voice tone. These motions are all amplified in groups that people are inexperienced with (Fiske, 2002).

In later research Babad and colleagues (1991) showed that students of all ages respond to both the verbal and non-verbal behaviour of teachers. In this study, teachers would verbally relay how they felt about their students to researchers. Although they tried not to betray these feelings to their students, the students were able to pick up on the non-verbal cues and used these as a tell for how their teachers expected them to perform academically. Thus, students based their expectations of themselves upon these cues.

When stating you are an equitable, non-biased, 'not racist' teacher who treats all students the same, this could be simultaneously true of your verbal communication but the opposite for your non-verbal communication. As a teacher your subconscious actions in the classroom will reveal your expectations of and feelings about your students.

### Reflection

The next time you are talking to a Student of Colour, think about your body language.

1.   How are you holding yourself?
2.   Are you looking them in the eye?
3.   Are your arms crossed or open, are you facing them?

Try to consciously think about what your body language is doing and how you can improve it.

## What Is the Impact of Teacher Bias on Students?

Self-efficacy is a measure of an individual's belief in their capacity to execute behaviours necessary to produce specific performance outcomes (Bandura, 1977, 1986, 1997). The greater the students' belief that they

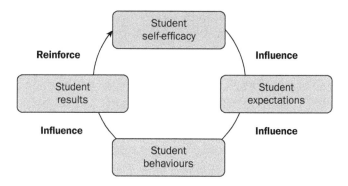

**Figure 4.1**   How does self-efficacy impact our students?

can do a task well, the better they will perform. Students who value their work and believe they have competence in the tasks are more motivated and as a result perform better. When teachers believe their students can succeed (academically) and value the knowledge they are teaching, this belief is contagious and infects their students with a higher sense of self-efficacy.

One of the facets of low self-efficacy (and high self-doubt) is that it has an impact on resilience through cognitive, motivational and affective decision-making processes. Your students are more likely to see the futility of their ability to change their predicament when faced with challenges; this detrimentally hampers aspirations through lowering expectations of their abilities (Bandura, 1997, p. 4). Inversely, those with high self-efficacy can picture successful scenarios and stay positive about their abilities (Bandura, 1993).

You can see the obvious process which leads to low (or high) self-efficacy. This process is complete when the outcomes match up to what the student originally predicted for themselves. Thus the very existence of the prophecy sets the course for outcome of events.

> If men define situations as real, they are real in their consequences. (W. I. Thomas, in Merton, 1948, p. 193)

## Internal Self-fulfilling Prophecy

**A Positive Loop:**
- Prophecy: I am going to get good grades in science.
- Self-efficacy: I love science, I'm really good at it.
- Self-expectations: I expect to get the top grades.
- Behaviours: I will revise harder and longer to make sure it happens.

- Results: Grades are higher because of the prior actions and this reinforces the self-efficacy and round and round we go.

**A Negative Loop:**
- Prophecy: I am going to fail science.
- Self-efficacy: I hate science, I can't do it.
- Self-expectations: I don't care about science, I'll do what I can.
- Behaviours: I will try to revise, I obviously don't get it, what's the point?
- Results: Grades are lower because of the prior actions and this reinforces the low self-efficacy and round and round we go.

## How Do Teachers Fit Into the Machine?

Teacher bias and expectations are essentially cogs and gears of the 'self-fulfilling' prophetic machine. Students absorb their teachers' expectations into their own self-efficacy, which causes lower or higher outcomes, which in turn reinforces both the students' and the teachers' original beliefs and the cycle continues. Whether consciously or subconsciously we expect Pupils of Colour to perform differently from their counterparts so that's what happens, and the whole cycle rolls on. It was found that the most vulnerable students are most at risk of this phenomenon, and that

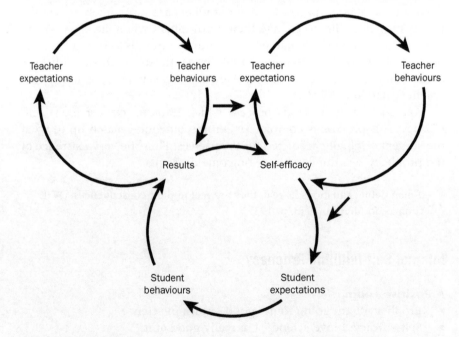

**Figure 4.2** Teachers' and students' behaviour and expectations interact to have a tangible impact on results

self-fulfilling prophecies are more powerful when they are negative as opposed to positive (Jussim et al., 1987). So, it follows that self-fulfilling prophecies are more powerful for lower achievers (who we would assume are more prone to the negative loops). When teachers have higher expectancies of low-ability students, there is a greater chance of them getting better grades in assessments (Madon et al., 1997). Teacher expectations – and thus bias – drive the whole machine. We can either continue to move the machine foward or stop it in its tracks.

---

## Reflection

It is time for you to be honest with yourself.

1.  How do you perceive and treat Students of Colour?
2.  Do you treat students from different minority ethnic backgrounds differently from the white students in your classroom?
3.  Do you have different expectations for white students and different groups of Black and minority ethnic students in your classroom?

---

# Marking and Outcomes – Deficit Thinking

We have to recognise that most school systems are based on what is known as a deficit thinking model. This is the idea that students are assumed to start the school year with the potential of achieving 100% in their assessment, but through loss of learning this percentage will drop as a result. For example, if a student is consistently missing days of schooling they are likely to miss out on the content that will appear in exam papers. This is the modus operandi of schools in the UK. Our system seeks to measure what our students don't know. We could be doing the opposite. Why not assess through a method which shows off what a student has actually learned? An assessment system which doesn't tell us what a student has learned currently moves away from the aim of learning and to the aim of passing the exam. This has led to teachers organising lessons and schemes of learning around assessment objectives, in addition to scores of educators teaching exam literacy, which has no purpose other than to mould students to be able to pass exam papers.

## Assessment Is Subjective

Marking is not an objective process; even in subjects like maths, where you'd expect near faultless accuracy between A-level and GCSE exam markers and principal examiner, discrepancies exist. Four out of 100 scripts would receive a different grade if marked by a more experienced marker. In subjective essay style subjects (such as English Literature, Religious Studies and History), the average probability of a match lies between 55% and 60%; that wasn't a typing error. 45 entries out of 100 would receive a different grade when moderated (Keating, 2019).

## Examples of Marking Bias

Let's look at the exams themselves. Even though external exams themselves are biased (through a multitude of issues such as ethnocentric questioning and marking biases), and so are not a perfect measure of students' ability, trends in ethnic and racial groups do still exist. As it stands, when we marry this with the evidence of teachers' racial bias, we have a toxic family of outcomes. The same processes which lead to self-fulfilling prophecies and the consequent Rosenthal effect mean that even with this variability in exam marking, external examiners are still a better judge of achievement for Black and Brown students. Systemically, Students of Colour nearly always do better in their exams compared to their teachers' assessments of their ability.

Let us take a look at some quantitative data. David Burgess and Ellen Greaves (2009) compared teacher assessment to actual attainment in external exams of 11-year-olds across 16,557 schools, 3 subjects (English, Maths and Science) and 4 years. Burgess and Greaves present the following data for year 6 SATS.

In English, all students who do not fall in the white group have a higher percentage of their teachers assessing them lower than they achieve in their external test. Pakistani students are under assessed (vs their external SATS grade) when compared with white students at a rate of 62.9%. That means it is 62.9% more likely for your teacher to think you are working at a level below what you actually achieve in a high-stress external exam. Similar patterns and trends are shown for maths and science, with the exception of Chinese students in maths and science, where teacher bias points towards the positive (remember these trends are damaging for everyone, whether positive or negative).

That data is hard to swallow; you may be thinking that you don't assess your students based on their skin colour. Honestly, I want to believe you, but have you ever checked? Have you looked over your teacher assessments and compared them to external results? Even if you have and there is no difference between racial groups, we can't deny that systemic discrimination is prevalent nationally. Luckily schools are data-rich environments. As practitioners you are likely to be able to look at your assessments and external results reaching back decades. This self-interrogation requires courage and bravery. You must be prepared to discover that you are part of the system that upholds the structures which lead to the denigration of life chances for Students of Colour. Senior and middle leaders, please note that this type of simple analysis is extremely helpful in identifying subject- and teacher-specific anomalies.

## Where it Starts

School children are assessed throughout the early years' foundation phase and key stage 1 through a variety of different methods but it is only at the climax of key stage 2 that students are assessed externally. So, it is likely that this underassessment (and its consequences) exists day-to-day in the classroom, but it is unlikely to be even acknowledged in the first 11 years of a child's life. Wilson et al. (2011) tracked two cohorts across schools against assessments. In school the assessment of all Black groups decreases between the ages of 7 and 14 relative to white students.

Their research presents that Black African, South Asian groups and Chinese students perform better than white students during key stages 2–4. This is not the case with Black other and Black Caribbean categories in terms of raw attainment; however, the quantitative and systemic reality is that all Students of Colour make more progress than their white counterparts through secondary schooling.

What are the reasons for the leap in progress for Students of Colour at 16? I remember sitting in a lecture theatre at the London School of Economics in 2019 at the 'Racial Inequality in Britain: The Macpherson Report 20 Years On' event. I felt my stomach drop as Dr Faiza Shaheen from the CLASS think tank stated the steep rise at age 16 for Black British African and Caribbean students was because this is the first time in our students' school journey that they are assessed completely anonymously.

## Teachers Underassess Students to Motivate Them

We all know our students and some of them need a shock to understand the consequences of their actions. This can have an impact on students both positively and negatively. This justification for underassessment has some merit and is empirically tested.

Hvidman and Sievertsen (2021) studied a Danish reform which led to some students' grades being recoded and ultimately their GPA scores (Grade Point Average) being downgraded. This led to students reducing their paid work and probably investing that extra time into study; they found that students who were downgraded performed better on subsequent assessments, indicating the importance of incentives. An argument to keep the current system is that these students react more positively to predicted grades. However, this doesn't answer the question of why this underassessment would be utilised in greater proportions with Students of Colour than white ethnic groups in the years before the external examinations.

## 'Students of Colour go to worse schools'

> Over the country as a whole, attendance at substantially mono-ethnic schools is not the norm for members of the non-white groups (though it is for whites in many areas). Half of all non-white secondary students in England attended schools where more than 75 per cent of the total enrolment comprised whites. (Johnston et al., 2004)

That means that in the UK, BAME students are not segregated (nationally) as Students of Colour go to a wide range of schools, so, in the main, this cannot be a huge factor in the trend.

## Language Acquisition

Students whose primary language is not English who are still learning English achieve lower than expected levels in primary school terminal exams. As these students become more and more proficient in the language, their attainment in school assessments increases. Demie and Strand (2006) found that at 10 secondary schools in the London Borough of Lambeth bilingual students who were proficient in English on average performed significantly better than their solely English-speaking peers; although we have to recognise that when a regressive analysis is undertaken this effect becomes non-statistically significant. It would be rational to expect there to be large variations between maths and English in terms of attainment, due to maths using fewer words than English. Unfortunately Wilson et al. (2011) found that in the national dataset this simply isn't the case. They also found that students with English as an additional language were found to have on average around 0.9 extra GCSE points; both EAL (English as an Additional Language) and non-EAL Students of Colour gain 3.0 GCSE points when compared to white students. All in all, Wilson et al. (2011) suggest that the impact of language acquisition accounts for up to a third of BAME performance improvement at key stage 4. This means that two-thirds of the increase is still unaccounted for.

## Ethnocentric Testing

Ethnocentrism is the act of centring the gaze on the dominant culture. If the lessons are based on a culture that is far away from your own, you will be disadvantaged as a result. The assessment then becomes about how well you know that culture and not about the learning of the skills and knowledge. There are many arguments around ethnocentric testing typically working against Black students and poorer students (Burgess and Greaves, 2009). I wholly agree there are real issues with the content of external assessments; logically, forcing students into engaging with unfamiliar contexts has to have an impact. That process should cause their performance in external assessments to decrease but surely this would lead to teachers inflating students' assessments over the external examination? This is not the case in the data as the inverse is true.

## The Consequences of Systemic Discrimination in Assessment

Researching the data, gut-wrenchingly similar trends are repeated in further assessments in primary schools. Pupils have a smaller probability of their teacher rating them as 'above average' in reading if they are boys, SEND (special educational needs and/or disabilities), Bangladeshi, Pakistani, Indian, Black African and Black Caribbean, EAL students and come from lower income families (Campbell, 2015). All Pupils of Colour seem to suffer when analysing reading scores. Bangladeshi and Pakistani pupils are around 16% less likely to be assessed as above average reading by their teachers when compared to their white counterparts with the equivalent scores on the word reading test; inversely they are 12.8% and 8.6% more likely to be assessed as being below average.

Wilson et al. (2011) demonstrated the difference in key stage 2 teacher assessment extrapolated to GCSE, versus actual grades at GCSE using white students as the comparison. This impact is significant as the figures for most groups are vastly different in the positive direction. The data further reinforces the idea that racial biases in assessment exist, and that Students of Colour systemically achieve despite what their teachers think of them and expect of them.

---

### Reflection

Questions to ask yourself:
1.   Why do Black Caribbean and Black Other British students buck this trend?
2.   What happens in our secondary schools which causes these groups to underachieve based on an already biased primary experience?
3.   In your context which groups follow these patterns and which do not?

---

How can we as teachers fulfil our duty to educate and empower all our students, pushing them to the best of their ability if we have trouble

**Table 4.1**  Predicted vs. actual KS4 attainment by ethnicity

| Ethnicity | Actual percentage of pupils obtaining 5 or more A*–Cs at KS4 | Predicted percentage of pupils obtaining 5 or more A*–Cs at KS4[a] |
|---|---|---|
| Black African | 48.24% | 39.22% |
| Black Caribbean | 32.55% | 38.76% |
| Black Other | 38.06% | 41.91% |
| Bangladeshi | 47.98% | 35.67% |
| Indian | 64.97% | 47.98% |
| Pakistani | 41.57% | 32.30% |
| Chinese | 76.25% | 58.76% |
| Other | 53.93% | 49.28% |
| White | 52.68% | 52.68% |

[a]*Percentage* of pupils attainment 5 or more A*-Cs at KS4 is predicted by running a logit of whether pupil attains 5 or more A*-Cs on overall KS2 score and gender for White pupils only.

*Source*: Burgess and Greaves, Test Scores, Subjective Assessment, and Stereotyping of Ethnic Minorities, *Journal of Labor Economics* Volume 31 (3) © 2013 by The University of Chicago. Reprinted by permission of The University of Chicago Press.

assessing where Black and minority ethnic students actually are? These huge nationwide studies throw up the consequences of stereotype modelling by teachers.

It is always pleasantly surprising on results days to find that some students have 'outperformed' and 'pulled it out of the bag'. However, we must ask ourselves if this is the case, or whether the actuality is that educators have been underassessing some of their students for the entirety of their school life. An important issue to consider here is the long-term impact on those students, what their day-to-day lives have been like within the school system and whether it is likely they will have feelings of inadequacy that persist despite any consequent success, or in other words suffer from imposter syndrome.

Students of Colour are more likely to have their teachers assess them below where they actually are through a systemic process. The data in secondary schools is harder to assess on the national level due to the way we gather GCSE and A-level data. However, there is no reason why teachers of secondary school students will be able to assess with greater accuracy; this is certainly not the case in my experience. Even those students who are lucky enough to have teachers who have real skills in removing bias and assessing more accurately, they are still held back as they are more likely to have the expectations of them tempered due to underassessment in previous phases.

The endless underassessment leads to teachers and leaders confirming their existing biases through target setting, placing students in sets, and so on, causing their students to be caught in self-fulfilling prophecy loops.

## Placing Students in Sets

Before we interrogate setting and its effects on Students of Colour it is worth noting that there exists a vast library of literature that shows that the process is inherently unfair and inequitable for the majority. Setting favours those in the 'higher streams/sets' a little and disadvantages those in the 'lower streams/sets' significantly (Boaler, 1997; Marks, 2011, 2013; Nunes et al., 2009; Slavin, 1990). This is particularly seen in the way lower sets place limitations and decrease the chances of pupils being challenged in their learning compared to their counterparts in higher sets (Archer et al., 2018).

> Research not only shows some persistent patterns of poor educational outcomes for students from low socio-economic groups, minority ethnic groups and boys; studies also indicate differentiated experiences of schooling and the over-representation of these groups in low attainment sets. (Muijs and Dunne, 2010, p. 393)

As educators we all know that the emphasis changes from profound inspirational teaching and learning, towards a mechanical outcomes-based delivery depending on the sets students are taught in. This is reinforced by the evidence that teachers believe that more academic students (in higher ability sets) receive a more stimulating and challenging curriculum and less academic pupils are given a more content-centred approach with the aim to equip them with the skills and knowledge to pass exams (Spear, 1994). The intersection of class is also a factor in setting; Mujis and Dunne (2010) found through an analysis of postcodes a 'strong under-representation' from the 'hard-pressed' group, coupled with a 'strong over-representation' from the 'wealthy achievers' group in higher setting and the inverse with lower sets. We have to recognise that this intersection is racialised as those postcodes do not exist in a racial vaccum. One of Boaler's participants described the process of setting as 'putting this psychological prison around them […] people don't know what they can do, or where the boundaries are, unless they're told at that kind of age. It kind of just breaks all their ambition …' (Boaler, 2005, p. 141).

Poverty rates were higher for Black and Minority Ethnic families. Almost half (46%, that equates to 900,000 people) of all people living in a family where the head of household is Black/African/Caribbean/Black British are in poverty, compared to 19%, or one in five, of those living in homes where the head is White. This effect is compounded when persistent poverty was identified; people in Black and Ethnic Minority families are between twice and thrice times more likely to be in persistent poverty than those in White families. (Social Metrics Commission, 2020).

Muijs and Dunne (2010) analysed setting in maths and English across 12 local authorities in England and randomly sampled 100 schools, completing a quantitative analysis of the composition of their sets with a qualitative

**Table 4.2**   Racial/ethnic group against representation in low, middle and high sets

|  | Sample% | Low sets% | Middle sets% | High sets% |
|---|---|---|---|---|
| White | 55.3 | 57.4 | 48.9 | 61.5 |
| Bangladeshi | 18.3 | 18.7 | 23.9 | 12.1 |
| Pakistani | 10.3 | 9.1 | 10.2 | 11.2 |
| Indian | 7.1 | 6.6 | 6.4 | 8.2 |
| Black Caribbean | 6.0 | 6.9 | 6.5 | 4.3 |

*Source*: Muijs, D. and Dunne, M. (2010) Setting by ability – or is it? A quantitative study of determinants of set placement in English secondary schools, *Educational Research*, 52(4), Taylor & Francis. Reprinted by permission of the publisher (Taylor & Francis Ltd, http://www.tandfonline.com).

investigation into their rationale for setting. In their research they found that while white students are statistically significantly over-represented in high sets, Black students are statistically under-represented in higher sets. Across the Asian subset the only statistically significant result is Bangladeshi students being under-represented in the high sets (see Table 4.2).

Further research from Connolly et al. (2019) looks at 9,301 year 7 secondary students from 46 schools in England. They found that when compared to prior ability (at key stage 2 fine grade scores), Black students are up to 2.4 times and Asian students 1.7 times more likely to be misallocated into lower sets than white students. Looking at the misallocation into higher sets a similar pattern is seen. White students are twice (2.09 times) as likely to be misallocated upwards when compared to their Black counterparts and to the Asian subset at 1.72 times.

## What Are the Criteria for Setting in Schools?

Muijis and Dunne (2010) asked leaders to write a rationale based on their setting. Data suggested within the same schools there were interdepartmental discrepancies. In response to the question on what basis setting decisions were made in English, 22.7% of respondents specifically mentioned ability. The vast majority of other responses (72.8%) referred to attainment or test results, with 4.5% mentioning other factors, such as attitudes and behaviours as influencing setting decisions.

In mathematics, ability was mentioned less often than it was in English as a basis for decision-making (11%), as were behaviour and attitudes (less than 2.3%). By contrast, use of achievement and attainment data dominated as reasons given (88.7%).

This suggests that you could be in different sets in English and maths when you exhibit exactly the same 'behaviour', 'ability' and 'attainment' in both subject areas. This ideological dissonance in setting criteria also gives rise to yet more opportunity for negative experiences for Students

---

### ACTIVITY

What are your current sets made up of? Which groups are represented through the subject areas and the legacy of the school? If you don't have a culture of setting in your school it's a good idea to interrogate your own bias here, so ask yourself who are the highest performing students in your school over time.

What is the make-up of high-performing pupils in your school?

1.
2.
3.
4.
5.

What are the attributes you look for in these typically high-performing students?

1.
2.
3.
4.
5.

---

of Colour. In addition to Students of Colour already being subjected to lower expectations based on previous assessments, their setting is also then based on ability, attitude and behaviour which are dependent on the perceptions of their teachers. We have established that ability and attainment are prone to bias along the lines of race. What about behaviour? Do teachers react to and perceive the behaviour of Students of Colour as being different from white students?

## Behaviour and Assessment

Do we as educators really treat all our students the same when assessing behaviour? When students were perceived as presenting negative behaviours (like being disruptive), their teacher lowered their academic expectations of them (Alvidrez and Weinstein, 1999). Having a poor behaviour profile affects teachers' ability to assess students academically. I can hear you, yes, I can hear you, the cynics among you are crying out 'well, that's part and parcel of life; behave badly and there are consequences'. Maybe, possibly, I would agree. However, this impact is also racialised: 'In summary, whilst the survey data shows that student behaviours and attitudes do have an influence on the likelihood of under-assessment, such adverse behaviours are if anything more common among white students' (Burgess and Greaves, 2009, p. 23).

It is likely that the stimulus for negative behaviours by ethnic minority students is not only provided by the Rosenthal effect, but also by teachers lowering their academic expectations even further based on their (racially biased) perception of this behaviour. Your teachers may expect you to be at a lower academic level than where you actually are (based on your race, ethnicity and class). This leads to a poorer experience in the classroom which elicits more negative behaviours more likely to be observed and to be exaggerated in these groups through the perception of educators. Both in turn decrease teachers' ability to assess students academically and we are very quickly caught in a negative self-efficacy cycle as well as a self-ful-filling prophecy of 'I can't do school' and 'I am always getting into trouble.'

## Do Your Students Trust You?

Do your students trust you? I ask that genuinely: do our students trust us? Do they believe you have their best interests at heart? What have we done to earn that trust? Without trust all relationships will become strained. The constant process of interrogating whether people have your best interests at heart as a student is exhausting. When a Student of Colour receives criticism from their teachers this may boil down to the question 'Does this person actually care about me or is this more of the same?'

## Reflection

1.  Which students respond to your feedback in the most positive way?
2.  Which students actively engage in the discourse around their learning and their work?
3.  Who reattempts their work and drives for improvement?
4.  Who rejects the red, green, purple – pick any shade you want coloured comments and who just wants to turn the page and move on?

### Building Trust – Wise Feedback

Trust has the impact of allowing students to separate the motives of criti-cism as information to improve themselves from the evidence that bias exists (Yaeger et al., 2013).

We know that engagement, exam outcomes and belonging can be casu-alties of systemic racism, but these all stem from the murder of some-thing more important. I would also suggest that this funeral is the most important factor in any act of pedagogy: the death of trust. After nearly two decades in the classroom I have found that there are multiple forms of assessment and feedback. We have spent hours investing in different methods of feedback – formative, summative, verbal, dialogic, diagnostic, etc. But we need to be aware that no matter what methodology we use, there must primarily be an environment of trust. The aim of feedback is to elicit a motivation to be better and provide the tools to do so. When a student is brought up in a society where racial discrimination exists, they may, through social processes, withdraw in some aspects to protect themselves.

Children raised in aggressive contexts (which is arguably the case in the hostile culture of the UK) have a tendency to expect violence and may then interpret ambiguous interactions like feedback as provocations – which may start a cycle of retaliation and rejection (Dodge, 2006). Regardless of what you believe, Students of Colour will come into your classroom with different experiences and interactions with those in power than those of your white students.

With Students of Colour, if ambiguity exists between your intentions and your students' perceptions of them, this will lead to disengagement, lack of motivation and lower outcomes. Minoritised students' prior encounters with discrimination and their awareness of the significance of race, can affect their academic outcomes by influencing the way that they interpret ongoing school experiences.

## How to Deliver Trust?

I believe that all feedback has to be delivered with trust. One way of ensuring this is to take a 'wise' feedback approach; wise feedback is targeted feedback which conveys high expectations, the instructor's genuine belief that those expectations can be achieved, and provides concrete information to support the student meet the expectations.

Yaeger et al. (2013) investigated methods of delivering feedback to students by comparing the rate of response and outcome in:

- Providing critical feedback.
- Providing critical feedback with high expectations with the additional reminder that their teacher believes that they have the ability to reach those standards.

For the latter group critical feedback was supplemented with additional notes:

> Wise feedback group: 'I'm giving you these comments because I have very high expectations and I know that you can reach them.'
> The placebo control group: 'I'm giving you these comments so that you'll have feedback on your paper.'

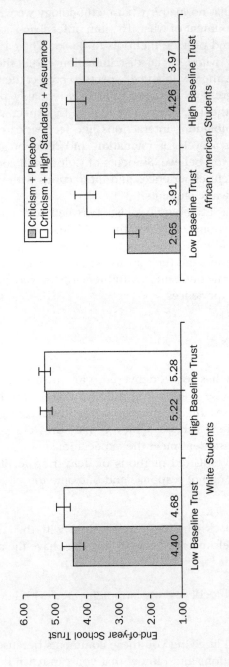

**Figure 4.3** The effect of making your feedback wiser on trust with white and African American students. Effects of accompanying criticism with high standards and assurance on end-of-year school trust (2.5 months post-experiment), by race and baseline school trust in Study 2. Values are estimated means at ± 1 standard deviation below and above the mean of baseline school trust (within racial groups). Error bars: ± standard error.

*Source:* Yeager et al (2013)

From the results it was evident that students in the wise feedback group were more likely to resubmit and receive higher grades when the feedback was wise. There was a statistically significant rise in African American students in both measures with a huge 55% increase in resubmission and over a quarter with increased academic outcomes. Using a logistic regression we can also account for the variable of trust. Low-trust African American students particularly benefit from wise feedback and this also showed that there is limited impact on high-trust African American students: 'wise feedback severed the relationship between chronic mistrust and performance' (Yeager et al., 2013, p. 12). The higher the mistrust for the school, the higher the impact on outcomes for pupils.

What is going on? Students of Colour are likely linking the feedback and criticism of their work to the racialised trauma they have faced and do face, causing them to question whether their teachers' feedback is because of the existence of racism. This may or may not be the fault of the teacher but that doesn't matter; this is not about educators. If you want the best from your students we need to centre on their needs. This one-off intervention corresponds to roughly a third of a grade point (standard 0–4 grade point average [GPA] scale). African American students who were given a wise feedback (one-off) intervention were significantly more likely to attribute feedback to teachers' high standards and assurance about their ability and this is an attribution shift that sticks. By the end of the semester, the intervention had closed the racial achievement gap by roughly 39%.

The idea of giving wise feedback to every pupil may look very onerous to the classroom teacher. I would advocate building a culture of trust, no matter what is written in feedback on their work. If your Students of Colour know that you are batting for them, that fundamentally they accept you believe they can achieve whatever is being asked of them, they'll go out and push those boundaries in response.

## Conclusion

Assessment forms a large part of the foundation of students' experiences of schools, themselves and society. Those three entities are interlinked and intertwined, and by changing these practices we can begin to disrupt the cycle. In my experience there is a common response of incredulity at assessments being impacted by race. You might think 'I don't mark my classes' work based on the colour of their skin. It's based on the work they produce.' I don't think there is a teacher in the country who would counter those sentiments. However, this happens, systemically across the country and, whether we believe it or not, we are part of a machine and we are the cogs that keep it turning. The impact of racial bias in our classrooms has a life-changing impact on young People of Colour. We must take heed to provide interventions that include their perceptions of their own ability and the expectations of those in authority.

## Chapter Takeaways

- Aptitude and IQ tests are geared towards whiteness. In creating targets base your judgements with care.
- Recognise and accept you have an array of biases. These are likely to impact on the assessment of all of your pupils. Incorporate the national trends and interrogate personal trends of underachievement and factor these into the assessment decisions.
- Negative behaviours are linked to teachers making worse assessments of academic progress. When marking, predicting or assigning grades, make sure you have factored in this possibility.
- Avoid setting as this is fraught with bias. As soon as you assert that ability is based on an arbitrary number/ranking top set, second set, etc. you are leaving yourself prone to bias and a student will likely adjust their expectations as a result.
- Using techniques such as anonymous marking reduces the opportunities for bias but, as bias is primarily based on expectation, by simply knowing the students who are in a set, assessing and recognising the handwriting will impact the process. Teachers are better served in recognising the issues and then ameliorating their impact.
- Keep your expectations high of all students and make sure you explicitly demonstrate this to your Students of Colour. Make your feedback wise.
- Use explicit interventions based around attribution and role models to interrupt the recursive loops around student mistrust and outcomes.

## 5.

## Racialised Trauma in Childhood

Racism is considered a fundamental cause of adverse health outcomes for racial/ethnic minorities and racial and ethnic inequities in health. (Williams et al., 2019a, p. 105)

## Introduction

Living in our society for People of Colour can be filled with traumatic experiences. These daily expectations and the experiences of racism may lead to low self-confidence and low self-efficacy, which can both contribute to multiple psychological phenomena. In this chapter we will introduce and explore how racialised trauma can impact upon the lives of your students and what you can do to be aware and alleviate some of this in your practice.

## What Is Racialised Trauma?

After the summer of 2020 and murder of George Floyd, I supported scores of People of Colour. All of whom were exhibiting symptoms of high stress and mental anguish. Many People of Colour struggled with watching a Black man being killed by the authorities charged with his care. An underlying issue that is often overlooked is that the impact of witnessing acts of racism does not just exist in the present but simultaneously brings back up a lifetime of racialised trauma. This is true even for Children of Colour of all ages. White folx reading this may be utterly oblivious to the existence of this type of trauma. People of Colour experience racism throughout their lifetimes, which may start with microaggressions and lead to acts of physical violence. Growing up in the UK, I have experienced acts of racism first-hand my whole life. I have seen people in authority inflict various acts of damage and violence to Black and Brown bodies intentionally and unintentionally in every year of my existence.

These experiences can lead to an underlying distrust in society and the belief that you must constantly be careful and protect yourself. Earlier in this book, we discussed that bias is built on repetitive responses to stimuli and that associations (shortcuts and habits of the brain) are forged for cognitive efficiency. Flipping the narrative somewhat, when subjected to or witnessing acts of violence, it would ultimately be possible that the brain would create defensive mechanisms to protect itself against those inevitable acts of violence.

These defences are harmful in themselves; we go on to discuss the impact further later; however, let me start now with 'hypervigilance'. This is a state where People of Colour are frequently forced into a place of anxiety and hyperawareness because of the risks involved in living in our society. This continuous attention takes up cognitive resources and thus affects all brain functions. Living with hypervigilance means that People of Colour are forced to constantly assess the environment for the risks it presents. As an adult with decades of practice with self-regulation, this phenomenon rarely even registers on my face anymore. Take a moment to reflect on how this could present in the young People of Colour we serve.

These consequences may arise from how our society treats People of Colour. A layer of mistrust is often used as an emotional buffer to protect oneself. In any relationship, a common belief in each other is vital. White educators may struggle to form relationships with Students of Colour because of their reticence to engage with teachers because of how they have already been treated. My father has always said that trust is earned and never freely given. It is not the responsibility of young people to trust our society; our role in our society is to nurture, guide and care for them to garner their trust.

## Racialised Trauma and Adverse Childhood Experiences

Before I go any further, let me talk candidly. When researching and reading for this book, I found many studies and articles that referred to disparities in 'race' and 'racial' differences. Racism has very little to do with genetics and is entirely socially constructed; it doesn't exist in the objective reality; it is merely defined because we as a society give it meaning. So, what impact can this have? It is not race that impacts health, education, life span, wages, statuses or anything else; it is racism.

Williams et al. (2019b) completed a literature review of nearly 30 empirical research studies on racism and its impact on health. They describe 'racism' as a 'dynamic societal system' that impacts the lives of People of Colour through stereotypes, stigma and biases. These factors may harm individuals psychologically, biologically and behaviourally.

A massive study by Felitti and colleagues (1998) screened 13,494 people for adverse trauma in childhood and compared the impact to measures of adult risk behaviour, health status, and disease. The adverse childhood experiences (ACEs) study by Hughes et al. (2017) used questions to ascertain if trauma was experienced (directly or observed) in the following categories:

- Sexual, physical, or emotional abuse
- Emotional neglect
- Parental substance abuse
- Parental mental illness or suicide attempt
- Violence between parents
- Parental separation
- Parental criminal conviction.

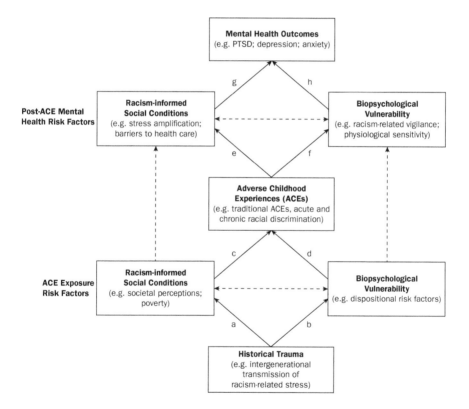

**Figure 5.1**  An adapted version of the traditional ACEs model to incorporate the impact of racism

Reprinted by permission from Springer Nature: *Journal of Child & Adolescent Trauma*, Making the 'C-ACE' for a Culturally-informed Adverse Childhood Experiences Framework to Understand the Pervasive Mental Health Impact of Racism on Black Youth, Bernard, D. L. et al. © 2020.

ACEs scores are the total number of traumas experienced and they are found to be positively correlated with stunted development across the board. More importantly the research suggests that adverse childhood experiences increase the probability of early death through:

- Social, emotional and cognitive impairment
- A physical impact on multiple brain structures and functions.

The impairment and physical impact increases the adoption of health risk behaviours (such as substance abuse, unprotected sex, etc.), leading to disease, disability, and other social issues.

What does this mean for educators? Of course, our students' health and life expectancy are our concern, but there are more immediate concerns around their school journey. In their UK study of 10,000 participants, Houtepen et al. (2020) found that ACEs were directly linked to lower educational attainment, as well as health risk-related behaviours, and overall health. Going through trauma as a child impacts the rest of your life, essentially who you were, are and will be.

Bernard et al. (2020) present an adapted model of the traditional ACEs model which incorporates the past, present and future. They have accounted for historical trauma, the impact of colonisation, chattel slavery, war, mass genocide and other race-based stresses. These events cause intergenerational damage, which is passed down through decades. Obviously, a legacy of trauma will impact on material risk factors such as poverty and the environment you are raised in, but also it will impact on the risk factors relating to the biology that People of Colour are born with.

## The Past

Researchers Racine et al. (2018) explored transmission of historical trauma. They found associations between parents' ACEs scores and poorer infant health outcomes, as well as childhood health and antepartum health risks (Lê-Scherban et al., 2018). It comes as no surprise that the parents are more likely to engage in coping behaviours (alcohol abuse, substance abuse, etc.) that impairs positive parenting (Meulewaeter et al., 2019), have a higher risk of anxiety and depression (Letourneau et al., 2019), and have difficulties forming secure attachments (Iyengar et al., 2014). As the ACEs questions include both personal experiences of and witnessing trauma so these parents, through coping mechanisms, put their own health at risk and in addition exacerbate the likelihood of passing on their toxic heirloom. All of which increase the ACEs scores of their progeny.

Thus the cycle continues.

The absence of specific racialised trauma from the ACEs questionnaire means that racism may bypass the ACEs pathway entirely and lead to the same inequitable health outcomes. The path leads to adverse health issues and early death through biopsychological and sociological conditions. Factors which encompass the social aspect of intergenerational trauma such as socio-economic status and perceptions from society are enduring. This means that groups who have undergone negative experiences are likely to continue to be in environments in which they are more likely to suffer further trauma. Racism is an atrocity or multiple atrocities in the microcosm of an individual's experience. We live in a world in which you are othered and ostracised for simply existing. We may not display the physical scars of our ancestors but, as well as living the legacy of their experiences, we also carry the burden of the racism we experience within our bodies, brains and beings.

Racial discrimination may cause dispositional biological changes in children (they are born with them). This world is stacked against People of Colour; even before we are born racism takes its hold on melanated bodies. Racism impacts physiologically and can present as stress-induced disruptions of immune systems, inflammation processes and poor cardiovascular reactivity, which are linked to foetal growth decay and pre-term birth (Davis and Sandman, 2006; Nepomnaschy et al., 2006). So much so that it can impact the prenatal environment through abnormal cortisol levels and lead to lower birth weights (Christian, 2012; Hilmert et al., 2014).

## The Present

Where racism and its trauma increase ACEs scores, it also affects the biology and psychology of Children of Colour as they traverse their education. Growing up with racism is a heavy burden, which comes in the form of increased allostatic (hormonal and nervous) response along with changes to their genes. Changes in biochemical and neural responses occur as children navigate their world.

Yes, I said genes. Our cells carry all the information required for every function in a human body; some will have certain genes which are turned on and others off. Epigenetic variations are changes in which genes are expressed. Racial trauma impacts the genes of People of Colour. It is worth recognising that trauma is complicated and although it is commonly conflated with single events, it is also a culmination of smaller more frequent effects. The drip effect of daily attacks takes its inevitable toll. The impact of racialised trauma comes from experiencing or witnessing harm, as both a distinct event (i.e. observing a racially driven murder or being attacked or racially abused) and as a summation of stress events, such as microaggressions and navigating stereotypes. Both are seriously harmful to one's mental health (Jones et al., 2016).

Microaggressions are small attacks, often unintentional and sometimes non-malicious. As educators, we must move away from making this about us. Intent is irrelevant if we are causing damage and these perpetual messages cause lasting damage. Table 5.1 gives examples of microaggressions.

**Table 5.1**  Microaggression against the narrative told

| Microaggression | Narrative |
| --- | --- |
| Where are you from? Where are you really from? | You don't belong here. |
| You're really articulate. | I didn't expect you to be well spoken. |
| You're not like the other ones | Your 'kind' are bad but you are good. |
| They ... | You aren't one of us. |
| I don't see colour. | Racism doesn't exist. |

# The Future

Racism affects the biology of its victims (hormonal, neural and epigenetic) as well as the social settings which lead to conditions like hypervigilance and the amplification of stress responses. Both of these strands culminate in coping mechanisms which lead to mental health issues which include symptoms of anxiety, depression, hypervigilance, suicide, low self-esteem and behavioural regulation difficulties (Cave et al., 2020; Himmelstein et al., 2015; Kirkinis et al., 2018; Priest et al., 2013). The physical and psychological changes are believed to result from prolonged and repeated biological stress and the body's response (Bernard et al., 2020). So, as people traverse their lives, the journeys to early death are powered by microaggressions, overt racism and implicit bias.

It's time for change.

# What is Racialised Trauma Informed Practice?

## Triggers

Those students who are subjected to trauma will have triggers and react to certain situations in ways which may seem like overreactions and irrational to teachers. In Chapter 3 on behaviour, we discussed the ideomotor principle (James, 1890), where simply observing and thinking about a movement sparks a more probable movement. A child who is subjected to consistent racial trauma or who witnesses their loved ones being racially abused will become expert in picking up warning signs. This heightened state of alertness, in which you are always on the look-out for potential dangers, is called a trauma response; it tells you whether to take flight or fight. While at first this may seem like a superpower, it isn't super at all. This heightened state of stress takes a huge toll on a person, both mentally and physically.

Here are some triggers that may cause a heightened response:

- Raising your voice
- Squaring up
- Staring
- Walking straight towards the student
- Towering over them
- Standing behind someone.

---

## Reflection

Think back to a time that you became angry in your personal life and you responded in a way that you wouldn't usually.

1. What were the actions you were responding to?
2. What thoughts where in your head?

Think about the last time you became really angry in a classroom setting; a time which led to you giving a pupil a detention, or sending them out of class, or making an example of their behaviour where in hindsight you would have acted differently. These times have happened to everyone. Go back to one of those moments and think about how you ended up there.

3. What were the actions the student took that led you to be in that position?
4. What were the thoughts in your head at the time?

---

Those specific actions and events are your personal triggers. Let me elaborate: shockingly, as educators you are also human beings. It's worth acknowledging your triggers and remembering that you too may react irrationally whether due to a trauma response or just a set of processes that brings you to that point. Dual awareness (Weininger and Kearney, 2011) is a technique used in psychotherapy where the adult is aware of one's present state of mind and is conscious of all the other events leading up to that point. The next time you feel angry at a pupil, take a pause and think about a way you can react which won't affect their triggers.

## Deficit Thinking

Have you ever said or heard the following from a teacher to a pupil?

> 'What's wrong with you?'
> 'Why are you like this?'
> 'I knew this would happen'
> 'Is this how you act at home?'

There is never anything ever 'wrong' with any human being and please don't make any links to the home life or culture of a Student of Colour. Remember your intent means nothing when we are talking about a trauma response. Let's flip the narrative. How about replacing the phrases and questions with:

> 'What has happened?'
> 'How can I support you?'
> 'You're good, let's have a chat.'

We are trained to search for students' weaknesses: reasons for why they may not respond in the way our educational system dictates. I'm encouraging you to look at your pupils from a different perspective. Rather than assuming there is something innately wrong with *them*, try talking to them on their level, offering support and see what doors this may open for you.

## Restorative Practices

Trauma responses exist in a world of experiences that many educators may not even begin to understand. The only way for the hormone-driven response to abate is to provide a safe environment where students can restore themselves and talk through their actions. I would be remiss if I didn't point out that the work here stems from indigenous peoples across the globe, where punitive systems are based on an aboriginal knowledge that leads to restoration.

> The basic concepts of (Native) Indian justice are relationships, reciprocity, solidarity and process ... [and] understanding that what I do has an impact on you and what you do has an impact on me. (James Zion, Solicitor to the courts of the Navajo Nation, in Malon, 2021)

Traditionally, indigenous courts are based on councils of elders, who work with parties to redress the balance. The real difference between these practices, the appropriated practice in schools and punitive systems is that this whole process incorporates the need for the perpetrator to be reintroduced to the community in a way that seeks to heal the damage caused. If a student acts out in a way that may be related to trauma, remember that this response is linked to othering, abandonment and exclusion. If the student who experiences these things decides to fight it, they need to be made to feel that they are still welcome and part of the community. This is the safe space we should have in our schools.

## Choice

A part of racialised trauma is the loss of control and the inevitability of a negative outcome (such as being undermined, targeting, violence, microaggression, etc.). In seeking to improve relational practice, think about giving students some agency. To assure them the outcome here is not inevitable, ask them:

'Would you like to sit down?'
'Would you like to talk me through how you are feeling?'
'What would you like to happen?'

Giving the students agency, a feeling that they are in control of this situation, can be incredibly powerful. In some senses, we all feel an amount of powerlessness in our every day lives, which can at times lead to frustration and anxiety. To give the victim of racialised trauma control can be restorative in its nature.

## Microaggressions

Remember the source of trauma does not always originate with a single discrete event, but often from an accumulation of multiple and frequent incidents. Microaggressions within the classroom or school environment for students can be a source of the trauma response. Just be aware that racialised trauma presents where othering is happening. Analyse the content you teach and think through the possible response to the narratives we promulgate. Think about the language used in interactions and in the literature and the resources you are using, such as textbooks. When thinking about the classroom environment you create, ask yourself:

- Is my classroom a safe space?
- Does what I teach foster narratives of the other/othering?
- Is the content of our curriculum solely focused on whiteness?

# GROUNDING EXERCISES FOR SELF-REGULATION – DR SARIF ALRAI

Dr Sarif Alrai is an experienced child and educational psychologist, anti-racist and Man of Colour. He has worked with various organisations across the public, private, and voluntary sectors, including primary and secondary educational provisions in both mainstream and specialist environments. He has also qualified as a cognitive-behavioural therapist, supporting young-people's mental health.

Teaching students to understand their reactions to stimulus, triggers and their responses is useful in raising awareness of the biochemical responses on show. Role modelling these actions is equally as powerful. Here are three suggestions for practising role modelling[1]:

ONE – *Using the senses* (use five of your senses to engage with the physical world/space you're in). You can mix this activity up as much as you'd like – the idea is to bring the person back to the physical space they're occupying. You can use five things for all of the senses or one. You can offer a bitter/sour/sweet to give them something to taste etc.

Name five things you can see.

What are four things you can touch?

Tell me three things you can hear.

What two things can you smell?

What one thing can you taste?

TWO – *Body awareness* (use your body to bring you back to the here/now). The idea is to bring conscious attention to the physical space and what somatic feelings are going on inside the body.

Start by taking five deep breaths – count to five while inhaling and seven while exhaling (do not hold the breath in the middle). You can do five in/out.

Next place your feet firmly on the floor. You can wiggle your toes (or not). Notice how your feet feel connecting with the floor – what sensations can you feel while you're doing this?

While sitting, stomp your feet (in tandem or not) 3–5 times. How does this feel on your feet/in your legs etc.)?

Place your hands on your knees – repeat the exercise about feeling feet on the floor etc.).

THREE – *Categories/distractions* (occupy the immediate thinking resources with simple tasks). The idea is to use up the cognitive resources to stop them from 'spiralling' and to occupy the thought process with a simple task.

> Count up from 13 (in 4s). You can use any number here, this is just an example.
>
> Name as many animals as possible starting with a particular letter.
>
> Spell a particular word backwards.
>
> [1] The following are generic exercises and were not invented by Dr Alrai.

## Learned Helplessness

As educators, we have all seen the impact when students don't believe they can achieve within a subject. I refer to this process as the 'I'm not good at [insert subject], so, I don't try, what's the point?' These statements are underpinned by a lack of self-efficacy and indicative of learned help-lessness, which will likely lead to a self-fulfilling prophecy. While we will discuss the impact of low self-efficacy later, here we will look at learned helplessness through a racial lens.

Learned helplessness is a psychological process in which someone accepts that an outcome is inevitable and does not attempt to alleviate the consequences, even when the scenario allows for avoidance or alternative endings. It mainly depends on expecting a result and believing that it is uncontrollable; the problem with learned helplessness is that this futility creates a cognitive deficit through the original act. So, relearning the opposite becomes more difficult (Abramson et al., 1978).

Much research has been collected from both animals and humans. One of the most famous was based on dogs, wherein researchers placed dogs in a pen with no way out where they were repeatedly electrocuted. When the door to the pen is opened and they can escape, they have learned the futility of trying and as a result they stopped acting and accept the shocks as a given. They have accepted and learned that the outcome is inevitable (Maier and Seligman, 1976).

Learned helplessness can present in humans as a failure to escape or succeed, which can move across to academic tasks. Glass, Singer and Friedman (1969) compared the impact of playing high-intensity unpre-dictable noises and similar predictable/more controllable sounds on later proofreading tasks. The playing of the distressing sounds caused a depression in results. The uncontrollable condition had the most sig-nificant negative impact on proofreading tasks and a propensity to lower subjects' tolerance to frustration. Later, in Glass et al. (1971), they describe the effects as being caused by the increase in a 'psychic cost'. It takes more cognitive energy to adapt to the uncontrollable loud noises than the perceived controllable condition. This increase in psychic cost leads to cognitive and motivational deficits (Abramson et al., 1978), which are transferred to other contexts. When part of your life is uncontrollable, and you feel the outcome is inevitable, the cognitive cost is so considerable that it impacts other tasks you complete. This belief may present as motivational and emotional, as well as cognitive symptoms such as stunted initiation and depression (see Figure 5.2).

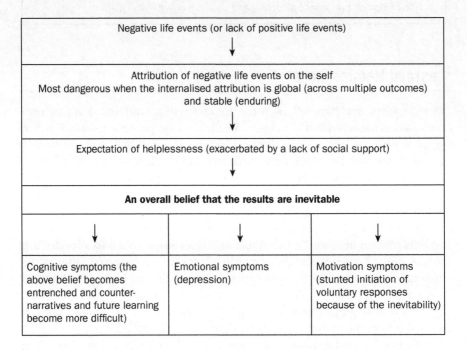

**Figure 5.2**  The process from actions, expectation, beliefs which leads to cognitive, emotional and motivational symptoms

*Source*: Adapted from Alloy, L. B., Abramson, L. Y., Metalsky, G. I. and Hartlage, S. (1988). The hopelessness theory of depression: Attributional aspects, *British Journal of Clinical Psychology*, 27(1): 5–21.

## Case Study: Learned Helplessness
## Contributed by Dr Sarif Alrai

So, we've started to understand learned helplessness as a cycle, a process by which we might start to learn the inevitability of our own failure. Prior to learning this inevitable outcome, we are in a state of limbo – an unknown place where the future isn't unknowable, it is predictable (I will say more about predictability a bit later) based on our experiences of the world around us. That is, the assumptions we will make about what might happen are not random. Those predictions are created by the way we have understood ourselves in the space we are occupying. Typically at this point you'll hear the example about finding reading 'hard' or 'challenging'. What happens if we find reading uninspiring or even unrelatable? Now, combine this experience with our relationship with our teacher. You start to see the logic of the examples given. Now, what's the significance of the word 'predictable'? The predictions that we will make will fit a particular category of outcomes. We have witnessed or experienced this previously so we believe it will happen again; perhaps to an even worse extent. All we need to do is wait. The waiting can cause anxiety. The anxiety feeds back into the cycle and perpetuates an increasing number of thoughts within the same category, likely scaling up in intensity. This is the learned helplessness cycle. Our outcome will be one of the ones that we are predicting, it is just a matter of time.

Take for example the case of Micah, a 13-year-old boy of Caribbean heritage. Micah was referred to the educational psychologist with behavioural difficulties. Wherever there was a kerfuffle or incident, Micah was never far away. He would regularly stand his ground/talk back (depending on your perception). He was regularly sent out of lessons and would often bunk-off the subsequent detentions. The narrative of Micah's presentation was that he was disaffected with his education, he was hard to reach, and that if this carried on the school would have 'no choice' but to permanently exclude him. Let's look at this situation using the two following questions.

- For whom is this a problem/who is this a problem for/who is the problem owner?
- Why did the school make the referral now?

Pause here to reflect upon the potential responses to these questions. Allow further questions to emerge from your reflections and think about why Micah presents this way. Think about what questions can be used to adapt the narrative to a more holistic understanding of Micah at school.

## Elements of Learned Helplessness and How We Treat It – Contributed by Dr Sarif Alrai

A crucial element of learned helplessness is that it is learned; anything learned can be unlearned – though some things are easier to unlearn than others. The active ingredient in this unlearning process is recognising that success is an attainable achievement when trying to complete the tasks required has been learned to be a futile effort. To create a more positive or enabling narrative for this process, try a process called Exposure to Success (EtS). Imagine for a moment that you're scared of heights, or spiders – or any number of things that your peers may or may not be able to relate to. Where your peers cannot relate to them, they'll tell you to 'just get on with it' or words to that effect – something to which you'll sarcastically remark that if it were that simple this discussion wouldn't be happening. Let's frame EtS in the same way, simultaneously simple and complex.

Another aspect of this learning process is that it takes place over time and so EtS needs to be repeated over time to become embedded as the new status quo. Imagine an elite performer in any discipline; think about what said performer's first experience of that discipline may have been. Unlearning helplessness and EtS are two sides of the same coin. We need to establish and embed this belief over time. There are various dimensions of learned helplessness: personal and universal are two umbrella sections, the difference being where the lack of control stems from – if this is attributed internally and based on the self it's referred to as personal and if it is attributed externally it's referred to as universal.

With learned helplessness the feeling of inevitability lives in both the environment and the minds of the young pupil, so any treatment should be centred around the ability to make a change to the outcome. To battle learned helplessness we need to first look at the sources of the effect which are split into:

- Personal
- Universal
- Stable
- Unstable

Personal and universal attributions are dependent on the origin. Stability is based around the nature of the entrenchment of the helplessness. The stable tranche is a continuous state of being, the inverse 'unstable' is more ocassional in its nature. Below there is reference to 'specific' and 'global' helplessnesses; this refers to the helplessness being discrete in one area or encompassing multiple areas. These are specific and global respectively.

Examples of specific learned helplessness are:

'I am rubbish at maths.' (Personal/Stable)
'I have a headache and I can't do this exam.' (Personal/Unstable)
'The maths tests that are set are always unreasonably hard.' (Universal/Stable)
'The maths exam is on Friday 13th.' (Universal/Unstable)

Examples of global learned helplessness are:

'I always get in trouble; this is because I am inherently bad and I can't stop what I am doing.' (Personal/Stable)
'I had no sleep and that put me in a mood so I am snappy.' (Personal/Unstable)

'The rules about my hair are unfair and unreasonable. I can't win.'
(Universal/Stable)
'The school rules change all the time. I just didn't know this was a
sanction.' (Universal/Unstable)

A real danger of specific learned helplessnesses is that they may become
global. So, 'I'm rubbish at maths' becomes 'I'm rubbish at maths because *I*
am rubbish, stupid and *I* can't achieve anything.' When this movement happens the impact becomes unbelievably vast as the nature of the student's
personality can adjust to accepting the pain of failure as inevitable and the
resulting behaviour is to lie down, give up and accept this is the case. Take,
for example, children who react to failure in an academic or achievement
context by giving up on further effort. Dweck et al. (1976) describe this as
a vicious circle of underachievement if not a broader pattern of depression.

Knowing what we know about the antidote to learned helplessness
and EtS, have a think about some of the responses to the examples given
above. It will be really tempting to talk *at* a young person trying to get
them to believe in themselves. This is the same approach as telling yourself
to 'just get over' your fear of spiders. Within all four tranches of learned
helplessness outlined above – personal, universal, stable, and unstable –
the narrative should always be that an individual can be successful or can
experience a level of success because there is something inherently skilful
within themselves, that they have potential and can train to be successful.
That is, the response to all of the attributions above should focus on the
practice and goodness within your learners that mean that they can only
control themselves and should put as much effort into that as they can.

It is important that EtS is a simple and practical journey. Start with
tasks that are already being accomplished to build momentum and
ensure that the next step is within reach. One risk of pushing too hard
too quickly is 'injury' which will cause a setback on your journey. Learning occurs in the space between what can and cannot be achieved without support (Vygotsky, 1978). Drawing explicit attention to this arena is
referred to as meta-cognition; learning about learning. You may not wish
to describe this process to your learners as unlearning learned helplessness or EtS. It may be better to refer to meta-cognition and highlight
the benefits in this manner. It is important any implementation of EtS
fits within the other concepts highlighted within this book such as wise
feedback and racial efficacy.

## Self-efficacy

Bandura describes self-efficacy as the judgement of one's ability to execute the course of action required to deal with prospective situations
(Bandura, 1977, in Abramson et al., 1978). While racial efficacy is a

version of self-efficacy described in Chapter 4 on assessment, there are obvious similarities with learned helplessness but there are differences in concepts and differences in support. When experiencing learned helplessness, a student comes to believe that no matter what their actions the outcome is already fixed and inevitable. Low self-efficacy is treated by supporting students with their skills and competency, while learned helplessness can be supported through restoring value to the student's agency (Bandura, 1977).

## Racial Efficacy

Racial efficacy is a specific example of self-efficacy. Both efficacies are influenced by: performance outcomes, vicarious experience and verbal persuasion.

## Performance Outcomes

Having positive or negative experiences may impact on a student's self-efficacy. If a young person has experience of performing exceptionally well previously, this may have the impact of increasing the likelihood that they feel that they are more competent and perform at a similar level with an associated task (Bandura, 1977, in Abramson et al., 1978). Are Students of Colour given the opportunities to perform well? With deficit thinking and teacher bias in assessment, even when they do excel are they told as such? Are melanated students given equal opportunities to perform well? Actually, the real question is: are they given equitable opportunities?

Recently I worked with an inner London school whose student cohort is more diverse than our capital's average 55% BAME populace. Despite this, the student leadership team, the head students, are almost always exclusively racialised as white (and 'middle-class'). The process is decided through a student-centred approach and staff evaluation; both are problematic. Although students voted and chose democratically to elect their representatives and teachers oversaw the process, through their oversight the legacy of the group was still overwhelmingly homogeneous.

Antiracist work in schools is often seen as taking away from white students. I can assure you that in redressing the balance this is not the aim. However, if white students lose out because the playing field is levelled that isn't unfair, that is justice.

Let's see how bias plays through the process. Those white students may be the most 'eloquent' and 'articulate' members of the cohort, and again, I am not suggesting we denigrate them for that. This comes from being given the chance to develop these skills. There is a two-fold issue here, that judgements are measured through those of teachers, and so it isn't that Students of Colour necessarily lack these skills, but that they are often overlooked and perhaps not given the same chances to showcase them. How is your school developing minoritised students' chances to excel across the board?

## Vicarious Experience

Simply watching other people's performance may lead to an increase or decrease of one's self-efficacy through a method of comparing and contrasting with their own acts (Bandura, 1977, in Abramson et al., 1978).

Can we be what we can't see?

Students may see other People of Colour succeed and they may even be role models in their eyes. In their teachers, the adults they look up to, the people they reach for validation, what are they faced with?

We have to start with which teachers and leaders students see. There is a difference in the proportions of students and teachers in BAME groups in England. In 2019, 85.6% of all teachers ascribed to the white British tranche in contrast to 34.6% of pupils who fall under the BAME label (Tereshchenko et al., 2020).

> There are approximately 451,000 teachers in the state sector in England, including 24,281 principals. Of the total number of principals, approximately 277 are of BAME heritage. (Miller, 2019, p. 988)

What is the impact on outcomes? Black primary school students matched to a same-race teacher perform better on standardised tests and face more favourable teacher perceptions. Gershenson et al. (2018) show that assigning a Black male pupil to a Black teacher in the third, fourth, or fifth grades (years 3–6) significantly reduces the probability of future high school drop-out and reduces suspensions (exclusions) (Lindsay and Hart, 2017) and improves school attendance (Holt and Gershenson, 2017; Gershenson et al., 2018).

## Verbal Persuasion

Encouragement and discouragement around a performance may influence self-efficacy (Redmond, 2010). People (teachers and students) of Colour as a whole have the extra stresses of society to contend with as well as the day-to-day of their lives. For example, it is not uncommon for immigrant cultures to pass on a 'we are guests' mentality to their children. The ideology assumes that immigrants are treated as outsiders by society, so, they must assimilate, conforming to the social hierarchies Do we encourage all students at the same levels? In all sectors of education?

## Conclusion

Trauma is a real part of the world we live in. For both adults and children, it forms part of their everyday experiences and, as educators, we have to be able to acknowledge its existence and ameliorate its impact. I cannot emphasise this enough; the effect of racialised trauma on Black and Brown students leads to early death and puts whole communities into intergenerational trauma cycles.

Racialised trauma may impact on Pupils of Colour through creating a lack of self-efficacy or more accurately racial efficacy may lead to differing states of learned helplessness, which should be treated by unlearning the processes that have brought them to that point.

## Chapter Takeaways

- Incorporate racial efficacy into your planning in every facet of school life.
- Expose Pupils of Colour to success where they have been trained to see failure.
- Consider the impact of trauma-inducing behaviours and the racialised factors, including the positionality of both teacher and student.
- Try grounding techniques with your pupils.
- Listen to your Students of Colour and let them know that they are heard. Incorporate racial efficacy into your planning.

# The Curriculum and Representation

Ignorance, allied with power, is the most ferocious enemy justice can have. (James Baldwin, *No Name in the Street*)

## Introduction

Curriculum can be defined as the content and interactions a student is intended to absorb during their time in school. I like to see the curriculum as a spiral or pyramid where the journey starts at birth and is built upon throughout our lives.

The curriculum gives students their grounding in today's society. What does this actually mean? With school leaders being subjected to a narrative of high stakes accountability, exam outcomes, while important, are not the be-all and end-all of education.

The word curriculum comes from a Latin root which means a race or the course of the race which is derived from *currere*, which means to run. Thus the curriculum can be viewed as a race, one that is multifaceted and sequential. Even though the prizes are given out at the finishing line, every part of the journey is important; the start is as important as the middle and end.

What does the racecourse currently look like for your students? What are they being equipped with? Do they leave your establishment with the skills and knowledge to access the next phase of their life?

## Schemata

Jean Piaget refers to schemata in his cognitive development theory as cognitive blocks of mental representation; these blocks are the basis of all learning (Piaget, 1976). We are all born with a set of schemata; crying, suckling, squeezing an object when placed in a hand, holding our breath under water to name a few. These schemata grow as we encounter new and different environments. Schemata develop in humans through assimilation and accommodation. Assimilation is the processing of the environment when it throws up a novel scenario which we put into an existing schema or schemata. For example: my god-daughter Ivy, when she learned the word for dog, called every novel four-legged animal she came across a dog or actually DOG! Her brain associated the new experience of meeting a cat with her existing dog schema.

Accommodation is where new schemata have to be built or older ones altered. I'm sure as Ivy grows her idea of what a dog is will change from four-legged and furry to being more and more complex, incorporating that some dogs have no fur or less than others and some may not even have a full complement of legs. These learning blocks are the basis of everything we notice, attend to and remember (Hastie, 1981; Marcus and Zajonc, 1985; Miller and Turnbull, 1986, in Padesky, 1994, p. 268). Thus, the cyclical nature and source of racial violence is laid bare; if the schemata presented are biased or negative the whole process is iterative and builds upon itself. This is especially troublesome when these toxic schemas are internalised.

Schemata help frame the world we experience. It is completely possible to create these frames unknowingly and for the reinforcement to occur throughout a lifetime without any recognition. Clinical psychologists understand that negative self-schema can be built and reinforced over a lifetime. Someone who has internalised schema that led to them thinking they are a 'bad person' will centre on personal defects, flaws, and errors, even when presented with evidence which runs counter and contrary to the original schema (Hastie, 1981; Bodenhausen, 1988; Beck et al., 1990, in Padesky, 1994, p. 268).

Racialised schemata are formed in many instances unbeknownst to the bearer. There's a similar impact on their ability to notice, attend to and remember. Over and over, schemata are constantly reinforced throughout the person's lifetime; for example, students see success in white faces and grow into teachers who notice, attend and remember those faces. So, the next set of generational and collective schemata continues.

## Collective Schemata and Internalised Racism

Collective schemata are the blocks of learning we share. As we live in a country with an imperialist past every one of us benefits from the trade of chattel slavery and colonisation. The rewards of our past come with atrocities that were and still are hard to swallow; the sugar to that bitterness comes in a reframing of the schemata, noticing, attending to and remembering through rose-tinted glasses.

It could be argued that this is not a conscious decision but due to the human psyche processing the positive more readily than the negative.

Subsequently, for example, nostalgia holds great power and it is easily manipulated to divert the narrative. In the case of the collective schemata, reality's rosy hue (or should I say white rose hue) becomes the norm and anything else is rejected.

These schemata are ubiquitous and exist regardless of the race of the bearer. The process of internalisation of racism begins to exhibit as a protective element with the aim of survival, an acquiescence towards the oppressor's history through the common curricula.

> In the colonial context, the settler only ends his work of breaking in the native when the latter admits loudly and intelligibly the supremacy of the white man's values. (Fanon, 1965, p. 42)

The French political philosopher and psychiatrist Frantz Fanon, in his immensely influential book *The Wretched of the Earth*, discusses the justification of the impact of colonisation on colonised people, and how their liberation is not a simple matter, as colonisers paint the native people as 'a sort of quintessence of evil' who lack basic values, ethics and are a source of 'absolute evil'. Liberating them from their and this 'evil' was the theoretical moral underpinning for the whole British empire. The frame – the British civilised the masses and taught 'them' the virtues of morality, 'gave' them infrastructure, religion and society – is a well-propagated narrative which may also be referred to as the Kipling narrative. And, if we hear a narrative repeated enough we start to believe it; we build the schemata, reframe and learn its validity. These same schemata make positives out of negatives for white students and simultaneously brainwash People of Colour through a process of internalised discord.

## Heroes and Villains

Mohandas Karamchand Gandhi is a personal and family hero; my Bapuji (grandfather) was actually present at the salt march. I believe that Gandhiji (the ji is added as a suffix to denote respect) achieved amazing things through his fundamental philosophy of ahimsa (non-violence) and that is worthy of celebration. Simultaneously and coterminously he held racist (anti-Black) beliefs and views. It's well documented that he thought of Black people as inferior. At a speech in Mumbai in 1896, Gandhi said that the Europeans in Natal wanted:

> to degrade us to the level of the raw kaffir whose occupation is hunting, and whose sole ambition is to collect a certain number of cattle to buy a wife with, and then, pass his life in indolence and nakedness.

Kaffir is an offensive term used colloquially in South Africa for Black African people, deriving from the Arabic for unbeliever. In an earlier open letter to the Natal Parliament (1893) Gandhi wrote:

> I venture to point out that both the English and the Indians spring from a common stock, called the Indo-Aryan. ... A general belief seems to prevail in the Colony that the Indians are little better, if at all, than savages or the Natives of Africa. Even the children are taught to believe in that manner, with the result that the Indian is being dragged down to the position of a raw Kaffir.

It is possible and actually more correct to appreciate the achievements of a person and simultaneously denounce the discrimination that they hold and commit. There is a natural tendency to protect our heroes no matter what; they are 'ours' and demonising their actions is like making devils out of the whole. Although life is full of intricacies and nuance, our society is steeped in binaries: good or bad, black or white, fat or thin, masculine or feminine, hot or cold, and heroes or villains; this leads to a knowledge-poor society. It is easier to put intentions, ideologies and people into boxes. This leads to a lack of critical thought and left unchecked this deficit paves the road to racism.

Within our own British collective mentality Winston Churchill is regarded as a national hero. The wartime prime minister triumphed against the evil of the Nazis in the Second World War and in doing so saved 'us'. When presented with this hagiography, I often question who is this 'us'? British people often refer to this collective 'us' as the natives of Great Britain; this grouping together points toward Von Mises' concept of collectives.

It should be well known that Churchill was responsible for the deaths of 3 million farmers (that is three times the population of the UK's second largest city, Birmingham) in eastern India (Bengal) in a man-made famine. I could talk you through the hoarding of food and the scorched earth policy but I think what Winston Churchill said at the time should speak volumes: 'I hate Indians. They are a beastly people with a beastly religion.' Does it sound and feel like I am lying to you? This is what our esteemed former prime minister Churchill had to say about the differences between Chinese and white people: 'Aryan stock is bound to triumph.'

In saving us, I ask again, who is 'us'? During the Second World War and up to 1949, all people with a close connection to the United Kingdom, such as members of the British empire, were regarded as British subjects. Millions of British subjects moved across the empire, fought in wars for king and country, and held up the whole concept of empire in every way imaginable. Black and Brown bodies were readily sacrificed for this idea of 'us'. Despite this, I spent a lot of time in my twenties explaining to people that my parents were born British, their parents too, and even their parents before them. I have often been told that I am lying about this. Although this is hard to hear, it is completely predictable when considering the way we engage in and as the British collective. So let me ask again, when we use the label 'British' or refer to this idea of 'us', are we just referring to white British people.

## How We Are Indoctrinated about the Empire

On 13 March 1919, the most auspicious day for the followers of the Sikh religion and a festival also celebrated by Hindus, immediately following the First World War, the British government enacted a set of laws known as the Rowland Acts, a continuation of repressive laws. A peaceful crowd had gathered on Vaisakhi (the Sikh New Year) in protest against the political imprisonment of vocal leaders against implementation of the acts. Let me reiterate *peaceful*. Brigadier General Reginald Edward Harry Dyer, with the consent of Michael Francis O'Dywer, was given the task of quieting the 'unrest' and 'restoring social order'. That day 10,000 men, women and children were gathered in celebration, and some in protest. Dyer ordered troops to block the only exit and, without warning, commenced firing and ordered troops to fire until they ran out of ammunition. Official reports state that 379 people lost their lives that day, with other sources reporting much higher casualties, around 1,500–2,000, the youngest if whom was six weeks old.

In a YouGov survey (Dahlgreen, 2014) during the Commonwealth Games held in Glasgow during 2014, when asked 'Is the Empire more something to be proud of or ashamed of?', 59% of respondents agreed with the former. I would ask how many people who engaged in this national pride are aware of the acts of mass murder committed during those times. Let us just pay some homage to the victims of Jallianwala Bagh and think of that baby, their families and the countless dead. And to the concentration camps and gulags used by the British (yes, you read that correctly) in Kenya against the Mau Mau people, where tens of thousands of people were killed and even more tortured (they won £20 million in compensation from the British governement in 2013; BBC News, 2013). I am more than aware that there are countless other injustices in our 'proud' history; I could go on for days.

In that YouGov survey, 49% of the people believed that the colonised peoples and their countries were left better off than before the British arrived. This is a reminder of the determination to reject truth and knowledge in an effort to present the legacy of empire as positive.

The Indian subcontinent was a global superpower in terms of world trade. Shashi Tharoor in his book *Inglorious Empire* cites the British economic historian Angus Maddison as demonstrating that, at the beginning of the 18th century, it was 23% of world trade, which is comparable to the combined figures for Europe at the time. When the British left around 200 years later it had fallen to 3%. I am not sure what the British really added.

Utsa Patnaik, Professor Emeritus of Economics at Jawaharlal Nehru University, calculated that from 1765 to 1938, the British extorted $45 trillion (Chaudhuri et al., 2019). Let me put that into numbers: 45,000,000,000,000 – lots of zeros! For more context, the UK's GDP in 2018 is estimated to be around $3 trillion (although there are competing figures, all of them are obscenely high). That is $681,818 per person for each of the UK's 66 million populace.

During British rule there was virtually no rise in per capita income in India between 1900 and 1946. Simultaneously, India registered the second largest export surplus earnings for the 30 years prior to 1929. After many years of British rule, the average life expectancy for an Indian born in 1911 was 22 years.

You may be feeling resistance to the above, even rejecting these facts; at this point I am regularly greeted with claims that financial aid is a form of reparations, thus the collective conscience is clear. However, British aid amounts to 0.02% of India's GDP; it is less than the amount the Indian government spends on fertiliser subsidies (Tharoor, 2017). I could go on and debunk many of the reactions that come from the dissonance, but here what we really have to look at is the nature of the reticence to engage. The rejection is highly predictable because, after all, we have all been radicalised with a set of schemata which relate to British benevolence and we naturally accept the narratives which reinforce these frames and reject any opposing ones. It's still okay for you to be proud. I am not here to change your thinking. Nor is it the job of an educator to tell their students what to think. However, without presenting all of the facts, in their entirety, this is not education, it is brainwashing. It's time to stop indoctrinating our students by giving them more than a fraction of the truth.

## Where Is the Time?

I am often challenged with: 'Exam boards hold the key to the curriculum; we teach what they examine.'

Why?

Now I am not saying that exams are not important, and even more so for Students of Colour. I would argue that they may provide an academic passport that facilitates students' choices. This, however, is not a zero-sum game.

Kate Hammond (2014, pp. 18–24) draws an obvious conclusion from her research of GCSE history essays: the link between the best historical analyses and those whose work was secure but less convincing was not determined by the content of the exam board's marking scheme but the size (and breadth) of the students' historical knowledge. Some of her students achieved high marks but were less 'convincing'. Although the achievement in these essays was high, it was simultaneously 'fragile'. She reiterates that the marking scheme did not provide the tools necessary to differentiate between her fragile top grade and her best students. This quality was not to do with the number of facts they were using to support their arguments and points, but a 'deeper quality' to the knowledge and being able to manipulate and use it in different ways, which she calls 'adding flavour'.

Her research led her to question the teaching approach driven by GCSE marking-schemes rather than by a determination to build a deeper and more wide-ranging historical knowledge. She states, in the same article, that 'substantive knowledge is "underpinned" by second-order knowledge and that substantive knowledge is needed as a base on which to "hang" evidential understanding'.

Here substantive knowledge is the knowledge of what happened in the past; second-order knowledge is the knowledge of the concepts, disciplines and procedures that allow the study of history. I see this as teaching students to become better at history. Schools should mirror academia and wider society. In those forums, being a better historian doesn't solely mean that you can pass a terminal assessment.

Academic historian Dr Steven J. Taylor argues that, for him, substantive knowledge is underpinned by the idea that candidates need to know what happened when, where, how and why. But the real understanding of the field is in the second-order knowledge; this is what should be taught in academia.

At school (substantive requirements) – candidates who know that lunatic asylums were established as government policy in 1845 and can explain some of the reasons why they came into being (overcrowding, fears of degeneration, medical interest) – would do well. But within the profession and the academy, second-order knowledge is king. There is a smaller emphasis on 'facts' – yes asylums existed, but those who think about interpreting their existence do better. It is about historiography – what have historians said in the past and why? So, the second-order knowledge fits into wider reading and understanding, and being able to trace that in the 1950s there was a positive approach: asylums provided medical care for the insane and, while it was horrific, it was still well intentioned. The late 1960s and 1970s change the narrative and see these institutions as places of social control designed to lock away the deviant. By the late 1990s historians are arguing that they are complex welfare institutions dealing with a range of needs. Thus history is as much about knowing the 'facts' as it is about understanding how others have interpreted them.

Hammond later concludes by agreeing that she felt the difference in quality of history essays by more 'successful' students in that:

1.  They held multiple pieces of substantive historical knowledge in mind and used them to 'flavour' the claims they made.
2.  They chose wider historical knowledge when constructing their arguments.

Though using a wider array of historical contexts and knowledges may not be credited through marking schemes, surely this is better for the students we serve.

I entered the teaching profession in the early 2000s and, increasingly, school leaders have emphasised strategies that lean mainly towards achieving exam outcomes due to a progressively high-stakes accountability culture. I get it, trust me, I get it. I have been there and I wholly understand this can be the difference between having a job and not. However, there is no trade-off here between educating with the aim of creating better historians (actually this extends to better mathematicians, artists, writers, scientists, etc., which we all are every day; Counsell, 2018), and exam success. Not surprisingly, that exam success is correlated with this acquisition of the complete knowledge. To build knowledge teachers need to have the skills to guide students' thinking to contexts that go beyond schools, classrooms and their cultures. Subject knowledge, while important, does not itself provide the skills to relate to interconnected frameworks that are not limited by the boundaries of the curriculum (Twiselton, 2002).

Now staying with history, teaching about the British history without the massacre at Jallianwala Bagh, the Mau Mau rebellion and countless other events doesn't just take away from an authentic truth and plant a false narrative, it denies our students the contextual richness of global knowledge and the multiple contexts to analyse the world around them.

## Teachers' Delivery

The curriculum should be directed by school leaders but built and delivered by teachers. Twiselton (2002) categorises three stages of teachers; normally teachers move towards becoming concept and skill builders through gaining pedagogical experience through a dialogic autonomy.

*Task Managers*: Through a self-identity which is heavily influenced by their own experience as students, task managers appear to mainly rely on a knowledge of educational contexts, where they employ teaching priorities that involve authority, order and 'busyness'.

*Curriculum Deliverers*: Teachers in this stage have a modus operandi involving a broader knowledge base than Task Managers. Curriculum

Deliverers' primary focus is curriculum knowledge. When working with groups of inexperienced teachers, it's tempting, as a leader, to put this at the heart of teachers' daily planning routine and core purpose. Learning gets lost along the way and makes the process more difficult. As Counsell (2018) states, simply distilling the residue of 'core' can ultimately lead to teaching being more difficult and be detrimental to the whole process.

*Concepts/Skills Builders*: Educators here take learning as being the sole aim of their teaching. Tasks are seen as important only in the context of how they contribute to that ultimate goal of a deeper understanding and its relation to the broader framework of the subject. This allows the expert teacher to analyse problems and seek out effective solutions. Selective encoding of relevant information gives the teacher insight which enables the better use of time and draws on the most useful areas of knowledge.

The aim is to develop yourself into a teacher who belongs in the 'concepts/ skills builders' group. This is where teachers adapt to the needs of the learner not the demands of the curricula, and is often seen when the curricula are centred around the child (in the early years foundation stage); pedagogy is adapted, planned and implemented on the spot.

Educators are also a product of our environment. There is a need to empower teachers to undo the possible damage that was done to them in their schooling. All teachers are charged with ensuring education is at the heart of what we do. If we are honest with ourselves, learning is and always has been more than passing on reams of rote facts (especially the rote facts that are selected carefully).

You may be questioning why I have talked about pedagogy and teachers' delivery in a chapter entitled 'The Curriculum and Representation'. Ultimately, this is the aim and source of school's purpose. For antiracism to exist in your school it has to be part of every element, as the propagation of white supremacy already inhabits those same structures. We must reframe the curriculum as a broad and balanced entity for the betterment of our students' learning, a view towards global equity, and their exam outcomes. For this to happen educators must take the lead in driving themselves forward.

## The Curriculum as It Is

Regularly I am challenged that 'my kind' are trying to remove white excellence and replace these great people with a rewriting of history. Genuinely, I rarely advocate the censorship of anything. Censorship rarely leads to change, and the hypocrisy of railing against a narrative of omission with a call to remove others would also be loudly heard.

**ACTIVITY**

Think about the last 10 people you taught about, either in lessons or as people who are inspirational and aspirational:

1.
2.
3.
4.
5.
6.
7.
8.
9.
10.

Now take a pencil and first put a straight line through anyone racialised as white in your list, then anyone you would gender as male. As the earth is made of a multitude of people with all characteristics our curricula leads us to the idea that while the 'in group' members were successful in every facet of academia and endeavour since history began, everyone else sat around and did very little. Yes, that is not only unfair but more importantly it is not true.

Around 20% of our world's population is made up by white folx; that leaves 80% being racialised as non-white (the global majority). Let me quickly take a slight detour here; 'non-white' centres white as the norm, but 20% is not the norm. Women comprise slightly under 50% of the population; this means your list, if representative, should include two white people, one male, one female, and four Men and Women of Colour (I have not included other groups here as I am deliberately using very broad strokes).

I'd suspect your list does not match the proportions of who we are. Is it that you believe that the people in your list are superior to those omitted? What are the related schemata that you have previously built? Regardless of belief, that is the message you are sending to your students. Representation is important and so is the nature of those messages.

## Representation

Now think about the narrative of your curricula: the story, the journey, the different legs of the race. How are the characters set up? Who is passing and receiving the batons? Who are given the roles? The power? The lines? And who are omitted? I know some of you reading this will be surprised, and some will think the achievements of white folx are just extraordinary and we should just accept that; this is the impact of our schooling system.

Darren Chetty, in his contribution in *The Good Immigrant* (Shukla, 2017) called 'You can't say that! Stories have to be about white people' and in his presentation 'Beyond the Secret Garden' at the Royal Opera House (Chetty, 2019), talks about his experiences as a primary school teacher of 20 years in East London. In both he presents the impact of the literature that is taught in schools on Children of Colour.

In the latter he analyses Frances Hodgson Burnett's *The Secret Garden*, where he points out that the story starts in India but by the end of the first chapter all the native people are dead. Now think about that for a second. That message is troubling at best. About the People of Colour, Mary says: 'They are not people, they're servants who must salaam to you.'

The proportion of school-aged children in England (in 2019) who fall under the BAME umbrella stood at 33.5%. In 2019, 6,478 children's books were published in the UK and 680 featured ethnic minority characters with 5% of them being main characters. Over the last three years, 7% of children's books featured an ethnic minority character (CLPE report, 2020). Children's books are eight times more likely to feature an animal as main characters than BAME people.

Darren Chetty describes a time in his classroom where he often encouraged his students to write stories and use the name of someone in their family as the name of the protagonist, so that they could draw on their own backgrounds and not limit themselves in the classroom, making the issue of race salient. He goes on to narrate that a boy who had recently moved to London from Nigeria listened to his instructions and used the name of his uncle. The boy was interrupted by a British-born boy of Congolese descent saying: 'You can't do that, stories have to be about white people'.

Although Darren had supplemented his classroom library with books with BAME characters and read them to the class too, his pupils differentiated these efforts as story-time books, not 'proper' books used in their literacy lessons. What impact does that have on Children of Colour? Children learn very quickly the rules of the game in our society. How to play school and what translates as good and what equates to not so good.

Author Chiminanda Ngozi Adichie (2021) warns of the dangers of a single story in her TED Talk, describing how a student who had read her recent book approached her and said 'Isn't it a shame that Nigerian men are all abusers'. She responded that she'd just read a novel entitled *American Pyscho* and that she was shocked to learn that young Americans were all serial murderers. In the same way it is ridiculous to extrapolate a negative trait and apply it to all Nigerian men, it would also be ridiculous to assume *American Psycho* is an exemplar of all American men.

In our lives we are the protagonists of our own everyday stories; if People of Colour are not represented in the capacity of all roles, how can we ever see the spectrum of opportunities available to us? Also what impact does this have on white people, who see People of Colour in limited roles and stories?

## Moving Past Representation

Although representation is important and many think that is the aim of antiracism, it is really just a small step on the journey. Recently a friend talked me through a children's book which included a Person of Colour! It turns out that it was Mrs Patel who worked in the newsagent. Yes, this book contains People of Colour but simultaneously it contains the same old tired and oftentimes damaging narratives.

In 2014 Michael Gove's reforms effectively removed *To Kill a Mockingbird* (Harper Lee) and *Of Mice and Men* (John Steinbeck) from the GCSE English Literature curriculum. The conversations about resistance to this action at the time were based around the removal of People of Colour from the curriculum and that obviously saw *To Kill a Mockingbird* as a story of antiracism. But, is *To Kill a Mockingbird* an antiracist story?

*To Kill a Mockingbird* includes People of Colour but it certainly doesn't promote antiracism. Spoiler alert: first, the story is narrated through the eyes of Scout, Atticus Finch's daughter, so the anxieties and feelings within the narrative are centred around white people. The story is full of dangerous old tropes; a white woman wrongfully accuses a Black man of raping her, reinforcing the aggressive Black male trope, and during the book how much does Tom Robinson, the acused man, actually speak? We have an image here of an aggressive Black male who doesn't have the capacity to speak. Then the well-known and powerful white women's tears come into effect. In the climax, the lawyer Atticus Finch fails to exonerate the innocent Black man, and Tom Robinson dies, but it's okay because the white man has won the respect of his community. I ask again where is the antiracism? All I see is more racism, its propagation and the message is broadcast loudly.

In Steinbeck's classic *Of Mice and Men*, Crooks (a Black man) is quoted as being the only character who owns books. How many times is Crooks presented by English teachers as being intelligent or well read? While he is faced with torrents of racial abuse, how often do we frame his character as resilient? There are many examples in our classrooms, Dickens is often heralded as a social reformer and it is true his stories often challenged the evident class structures in place. Yet while writing of social inequalities in the UK, Charles Dickens makes no mention at all of the existence of slavery at the time; what does this omission say? Not saying something often says something louder than we could ever scream it.

## The White Saviour Complex

Many stories are based on the white saviour complex, an age-old trope. Rudyard Kipling makes this the central theme of his 1899 poem 'The White Man's Burden':

> Take up the White Man's burden
> Send forth the best ye breed
> Go bind your sons to exile
> To serve your captives' need
> To wait in heavy harness,
> On fluttered folk and wild
> Your new-caught, sullen peoples,
> Half-devil and half-child.

Kipling portrays a world view that Europeans are, through their superiority, obliged to look after, save and develop People of Colour through a process of civilisation. The poem infantilises Brown and Black folx and requires white people to 'save' them. The absurdity of this narrative can be seen when you research indigeneous cultures, their longevity far surpassing that of white communities.

A more recent example of this is the film *Hidden Figures*, which is based on a true story. The story is ironically about uncovering the contributions of Black women to the NASA space launch. During the film there is a poignant moment of acceptance when a white man, 'Mr Al Harrison', hammers down a Coloured ladies bathroom sign with a crowbar and exclaims: 'Here at NASA, we all pee the same colour.'

Later in the film, he brings Katherine Johnson to the control room so that she can watch the rocket launch that she helped bring to fruition. What's the problem, Pran? This is a good thing surely? We have a true story, women, and actually Women of Colour and white ally-ship. Yes, representation and ally-ship is important, especially in 'true' stories. The problem is that Katherine Johnson actually watched the launch from her desk because that great white man, Al 'I'm pivotal to the plot' Harrison, didn't actually exist. Johnson, when asked if she used the coloured bathroom said 'I just went on in the white one' (Thomas, 2017). This is the trope; think back to all protagonists of Colour: when are they portrayed as doing amazing things without having white people there to help?

If we look at the curriculum as a culmination of narratives, school life can be viewed as a collection of short stories. In that compendium what would be the trends and tropes that exist? Ask yourself what the entire book tells you; what are the experiences of your students implicitly and explicitly? What is the character arc for the Students of Colour and the white students? The first thing to do is to look at the players in the book on a day-to-day basis; who is truly included?

The process of evaluation is difficult for two reasons; the first is because every teacher who has gone through the UK system has also been through the same colonised curriculum, so, our own views are tainted with this bias. If I were to ask you about great artists, writers, scientists, discoverers, mathematicians, doctors or any position of success, I would hazard a guess that the proportions would not be a true representation of the global population, or even the numbers of people in the joint history of the British empire.

The second reason is the impact of oppression on the world itself. Recently, working with an art curriculum, I was asked about female printers from a period of history and we found that very few existed. The solution is not to censor the topic but to teach our students the critical skills to ask 'why?'. It's okay to teach students that any homogeneous group held positions of success, but frame the context through power and subjection. We discuss creating a critical learning community in Chapter 7.

## Conclusion

The first step in realising the responsibility of education is to recognise the power we hold as teachers. It is our duty as educators to be better than those who came before us. Every single educator in the UK has undergone and participated as a learner in a colonised curriculum.

In our lessons, to disrupt this cycle we must seek to disrupt our own view of the world through teaching a more balanced representation of the world we inhabit. The framing of power is crucial; as educators our job is not to peddle propaganda but to strive to teach an authentic knowledge and give our students the skills to search out the same. I am not advocating an 'anti' British narrative, or 'anti' anyone else for that matter, but an ownership of the truth, no matter how unsavoury, enriches the lives of us all.

## Chapter Takeaways

- Spend some time thinking about those who you hold in high esteem. Think about their characteristics and then ask yourself why?
- Do the same with the students you have taught.
- Evaluate who is represented in your schemes of work/learning?
- Search out the power narratives in the lessons and curriculum you deliver. Who are being subjugated and who are hailed as heroes?
- Elevate the critical consciousness of the students you serve and incorporate their development in your curricula. Unless we give them the skills to challenge you and the system academically and ethically, we don't create humans but robots with limited capacity for thought.

# Teaching Power

Not everything that is faced can be changed; but nothing can be changed until it is faced. (James Baldwin, 'As Much Truth As One Can Bear', 1962)

## Introduction

Systemic and societal power can be described in various ways and through different ideological lenses. 'Power' in this chapter will be described through the definition of being a 'source of control'. Although this control may come in many different forms, we will concentrate on cultural, social, wealth and property. In this chapter some concepts that underpin worth and value in our society will be explored as creating environments where critical thought can be nurtured and taught.

What is the power you hold as a person and what is the power you wield as an educator?

## What Is Privilege?

'Being privileged' means that you are not denigrated and or inhibited in life due to a specific characteristic. Your earning potential is not impacted, your culture is seen as the norm, and it is likely that your social connections contain all the 'right' people. Growing up in the West Midlands in a small town was, at times, challenging. The 1980s were a difficult time for the working-class folx in our corner of the country. As people in our street all lived through similar experiences, to suggest that those white neighbours are somehow privileged may sound absurd. Yes, we all went through financial, material difficulties, and the consequent social dilemmas, but in being Brown, certain aspects of my upbringing were very different:

> *School*: A dumbing down of expectations, being told 'You're really bright; it's a shame you're not white, you could have been something.'

*Financial*: Witnessing members of your family being told they've got the job, but they aren't going to be paid the same as everyone else because no one else is going to hire them.

*Personal*: Being physically attacked while walking home from school.

*Career*: Being told to complete another writing exercise to check my English is of the required standard.

*Authorities*: Being incessantly stopped by the police.

Privilege is not a measure of what you have gone through but a metric of what you have not, do not and will not. Privilege is a definite lack of disadvantage. In the example of the above case, although we all lived similar lives, my white friends did not encounter the above.

## Who Are You?

Here are some of the ascriptions that I have chosen to identify with:

- Male
- Person of Colour (Global majority)
- Cis

All labels come with systemic experiences. Such as, People of Colour being structurally more likely to receive worse healthcare, with Black women in the UK four times more likely to die in pregnancy or childbirth (BMA, 2021; Summers, 2021). The lack of 'disadvantage' is what is known as having privilege. As a cis-heterosexual man, I don't have to regularly think about my safety; I don't scan the surroundings before reaching out and showing affection to my partner in public. If you don't need to worry about being safe in spaces it is dangerous to inhabit because of an immutable trait or have never needed to question or consider the impact of being there, you're probably living a privileged existence.

## Positionality – Multiple Characteristics

It is important to recognise that people hold multiple characteristics and will thus be both victim and benefactor, with various 'in' and 'out' group consequences. When viewed through the perspective of white supremacy, Black folx may be seen as worthy of pity, but when evaluated as competent they may become the subject of envy. The model, like power in its entirety, is not simple and unidirectional. As no one is solely Black, nor solely male, it is more complex than that. 'Complex' not complicated.

Yes, I am faced with systemic disadvantages, but I also have various privileges. It's a simple concept with many faces. Where these faces meet and intersect is where the individual experience exists.

Warning: here, people have a tendency to get caught up in describing the severity of groups' disadvantages and who is more privileged. I'm often asked to comment on who's more oppressed. I always question why this is important? This isn't a game of top trumps, this is not the 'Oppression Olympics'; all systemic oppressions are unfair. None of these disadvantages are deserved, just like none of our privileges are earned. If we are afforded a life without a disadvantage, then we owe society that 'lack of disadvantage' back. We should attempt to use our privilege to redress the balance and use the associated power to elevate the voices of those silenced by society.

What does your journey through life look like? Where are you systemically disadvantaged, and where do you lack that disadvantage?

---

## Reflection

Here I would like you to give yourself a point for each one of the following questions to which you give the answer 'yes'.

1.  Did you grow up with less than 10 books in your house?
2.  Do you occupy professional and personal spaces in which the majority of people are not the same race as you?
3.  Do you have to plan any journey meticulously because you are unable to access public transport unless the facilities are present?
4.  Do you have to look around and worry about who's watching before showing your partner affection in public?
5.  Do you fear or have you faced physical violence because of your right to choose your gender?
6.  Do you worry about being misgendered (through the microaggression of people getting your pronouns wrong)?
7.  To fit in do you ever try to change the way you speak?
8.  Do you ever worry about disclosing anything on application forms?
9.  Do you worry that people finding out your religion will impact their view of you?
10. Do you plan to leave a place before it gets dark because you fear for your safety?

---

I score four. It doesn't matter which four; what does matter is that there are people in the world who will have higher scores, some even getting a 10. What this activity encourages us to do is reflect more on our privilege and acknowledge the space we occupy. For those of us who are scoring less, we should use our relative privilege to advocate for those who score more. This activity should also help us to realise that not all societally determined disadvantages are visible, and to be aware of the myriad challenges that people with intersecting identities have to face.

## Where Does Privilege Originate?

Rationally in terms of power, privilege is a zero-sum game. To possess male privilege, women must be oppressed as a consequence; for a man to systemically be more likely to be hired than a female candidate means because he is advantaged she will structurally be disadvantaged as a result. Zeus Leonardo, in his paper 'The color of supremacy: Beyond the discourse of "white privilege"' (2004), expertly describes an analogy used by James Scheurich, who likens white privilege as walking down the street and finding that someone has stuffed money into your trouser pockets. Leonardo then takes it further by explaining that the money came straight from the pockets of the oppressed. Privilege comes from oppression; with advantage comes disadvantage.

White people may not physically take from these pots or even be aware of the impacts on People of Colour, but the damage is still the same, and so are the benefits. You may feel a sense of defensiveness rising in reading this. A typical response to this uncomfortable thought is to move away from the privilege being about power and dominance to intent. The intention is regularly raised in conversations about race, but this path is worse than pointless, in fact it's damaging. Any discourse on intent becomes no longer an analysis of power but a distraction, which then focuses on extreme acts of physical and verbal violence; this focus allows white folx distance from the damage they systematically cause.

Let us think of privilege as stemming from a set of endured patterned treatments of social groups:

> The experience of people of color is akin to walking down the street having your money taken from your pocket. Historically, if 'money' represents material, and even cultural, possessions of people of color then the agent of such taking is the white race, real and imagined. (Leonardo, 2004, p. 138)

In this quote Leonardo includes 'cultural possessions' as well as material ones. Later we relate this back to Bourdieu's three types of capital, the sources of control; racial privilege exerts a force, tipping the scales towards white people across power as a whole.

### Quadrants of Prejudice

The differences in interactions are based on the position of the quadrants in which the social group falls, as shown in Table 7.1. The larger the

**Table 7.1**  Common stereotypes, mostly based on socio-economic status and age, are shared across many countries. Other stereotypes vary by country; persistent stereotypes in the United States appear here (Bergsieker et al., 2012, Study 4; Cuddy et al., 2009, Durante et al., 2013; see link to individual countries, Lee and Fiske, 2006).

|  | Low Competence (Capability, Assertiveness) | High Competence (Capability, Assertiveness) |
|---|---|---|
| High warmth (friendliness, trustworthiness) | Common: Elderly, disabled, children | Common: Citizens, middle class, defaults |
|  | United States: Italians, Irish | United States: Americans, Canadians, Christians |
|  | Emotions evoked: Pity, sympathy | Emotions evoked: pride, admiration |
| Low warmth (friendliness, trustworthiness) | Common: Poor, homeless, immigrants | Common: Rich, professional, technical experts |
|  | United States: Latinos, Africans, Muslims | United States: Asians, Jews, British, Germans |
|  | Emotions evoked: disgust, contempt | Emotions evoked: envy, jealousy |

*Source*: Figure 1 from Fiske (2018). Stereotype content: warmth and competence endure. In *Current Directions in Psychological Science*. Reprinted by permission of SAGE Publications.

perceived threat from a social group, the greater the probability that a stereotype of unfriendliness will be formed because of feelings of frustration, tantalisation and annoyance. Even when out groups are perceived as successful, they may receive jealous respect for their skills (and control over resources) but simultaneously they are rarely regarded as friendly (Fiske, 2015; Fiske et al., 2002).

Those in 'out groups' who are seen as low warmth and low competence are treated with disdain and seen as parasites on the system as they do not compete in terms of status but are still seen as taking resources. Those viewed as the least competent are seen as in need of our pity and need to be looked after. As to the quadrant of high competence and high warmth groups, these are for the dominant 'in groups' and their allies. This final quadrant is where the summit of power exists (see Table 7.2).

**Table 7.2**  Warmth / competency against the nature of the bias

| Quadrant | Nature of the Bias |
|---|---|
| Low Warmth–Low Competency | Contempt |
| High Warmth–Low Competency | Pity |
| Low Warmth–High Competency | Envy |
| High Warmth–High Competency | Admiration |

*Source*: Adapted from Fiske (2002) and Fiske (2018).

## ACTIVITY

**Table 7.3**   Using the table above, interrogate the groups your colleagues and students fall into and the possible nature of the bias as a result.

| Quadrant | Colleagues and Students | Nature of the Bias |
| --- | --- | --- |
| Low Warmth–Low Competency | | Contempt |
| High Warmth–Low Competency | | Pity |
| Low Warmth–High Competency | | Envy |
| High Warmth–High Competency | | Admiration |

*Source*: Adapted from Fiske (2002) and Fiske (2018).

Being in an in group means that the higher your competence the higher the warmth towards you. We need to recognise that out group members can rarely win, no matter how competent they are. Even those with the skills deemed necessary for success are often seen as gaining them nefariously or in the wrong way through working too studiously and consequently lacking social skills.

## What Is the Purpose of Learning and Teaching?

Carnell and Lodge (2002) define a number of conceptions of learning. These are widely echoed in professional circles; they are what the learner is doing while learning is happening:

- Gaining knowledge
- Memorising and reproducing
- Applying facts or procedures
- Understanding
- Seeing something in a different way
- Changing as a person.

The role of a teacher is not solely one of knowledge transmission, but also that of an artist and a politician. I think every teacher accepts that in part we facilitate the passing on of knowledge, but do we ever interrogate our part in creating whole human beings?

Freire, in his globally successful book *The Pedagogy of the Oppressed* (1972), suggests that education in its current form is used to maintain the status quo. That it sets the scene of the narration, with the teacher speaking and the student listening, where the educator is positioned as a source of knowledge and the taught as an empty vessel for this knowledge to be deposited in.

We live in a social system built on white supremacy and oppression; those lines of power are seen clearly in our schools. We have a bank of knowledge which encourages not co-construction but which values the memorisation of facts. For any knowledge to be truly shared we need to move our thinking towards the creation of knowledge. Students do not exist as empty vessels but have a plethora of experiences. This interacts with the teachers, schools and classroom environment to create a new set of neural pathways. The transference of knowledge is never as simple as saving a document, attaching it to an email and sending it off. A better analogy would be to think of making something new, a collaborative act where everyone brings themselves to the table and takes away something slightly different.

Earlier in Chapter 2 on teacher bias we discussed personal construct theory around what we understand by words and labels; exactly the same premise holds for every facet of life. For a minute, let us consider what learning actually is. The teacher has constructed ideas and meaning around the knowledge they hold and seeks to deposit this through a variety of means. In that transference the student constructs their own personal meaning and the cycle continues.

Historically, teaching has been based on a system of depositing knowledge from teacher to student, and Freire refers to this as 'banking' (Friere, 1972). Teachers are the bank of knowledge that students make 'withdrawals' from and incorporate this knowledge into their balance. 'Banking' has been and is taught through a didactic method of lecture, dictation and direction.

Do we as adults favour this method of learning? As adults, actually as humans, in my experience, we rarely reach for the instructions. We construct understanding from our interactions between ourselves and our tools; even when wholly stumped personally, rather than follow rote instructions, we are more likely to reach out to other human beings for help, reaching for an opportunity to co-construct knowledge together.

> Learning … that reflective activity which enables the learner to draw upon previous experience to understand and evaluate the present, so as to shape future action and formulate new knowledge. (Abbott, 1994, p. 1)

Some of you reading this may feel that I am denouncing knowledge in its entirety. I am not. Whether we like it or not almost all learning is a social act (Black and Allen, 2018). Reading Paulo Freire's work in the form of the words in this book is a conversation between him, you and me. I may speak quietly and bring with me my past and present and he may speak a little louder and he comes with his self. This form of communication may be a bit one-sided but it is a conversation nonetheless.

A classroom should be viewed as a place where learning is seen as a collaboration: where we do not simply view our students as blank canvases. Appreciating this as an educator is vital for making change. For this to happen we must first appreciate our relative positions in the gallery. Teaching and learning should not be viewed as an expert-to-novice transmission. A teacher who feels they are the sole expert, who extols the contents of their brain and feels it is exclusive and exclusionary, has a tendency to accept no aberrations of truth. The student as a novice comes to the table with an existing vocabulary, an existing palette. In the case of race, Students of Colour arrive with a vernacular and range of brushes that many white teachers have never heard or seen. What we lose here is a dialogue of learning for all. Learning should be an amalgamation of these languages and colours; an appreciation of the mixing of experiences and without any amplification of the superiority of the white curriculum, standards and lexicon.

## Cultural Capital – Knowledge Is Power – Power Is Knowledge

French philosopher Pierre Bourdieu describes reality as being given meaning through the social experience. He refers to the 'field', which is where three sources of power are exchanged. For example, in an educational setting, we have the macro field, the school on the whole, and then micro 'fields' (Bourdieu and Wacquant, 1992). Examples of micro fields include staff meetings, the playground and the classroom.

Bourdieu presents the three sources of power as interchangeable pots, which he refers to as capitals:

1. **Economic Capital:** This is measured in terms of money, property and other assets.
2. **Social Capital:** A measure of social influence.
3. **Cultural Capital:** Split into the institutionalised, such as formal qualifications, and the embodied, for example, a person's phonology (accent and dialect). Embodied cultural capital is made up of the implicit unwritten rules, etiquettes and knowledge we pick up within an environment, and the objectified, which are material artefacts such as works of fine art and books (see Figure 7.1).

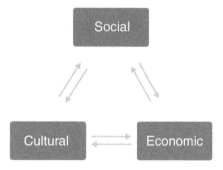

**Figure 7.1**   Bourdieu's three forms of capital

## What Is the Habitus?

Eventually, through constant interactions with the rules and the unwritten norms, the cultural capital impacts people's tendency to behave in specific fields. This set of behaviours is the physical manifestation of the embodied cultural capital Bourdieu calls the habitus.

Each micro and macro field contains its specific cultural capital; actually, all three capitals, which are exchanged freely. This is evident when we observe school leaders and teachers behaving very differently in the classroom, staff meeting and playground (see Figure 7.2).

This behaviour may expose the status of the leader, teacher or pupil in the hierarchy without any explicit statements. The habitus is not born

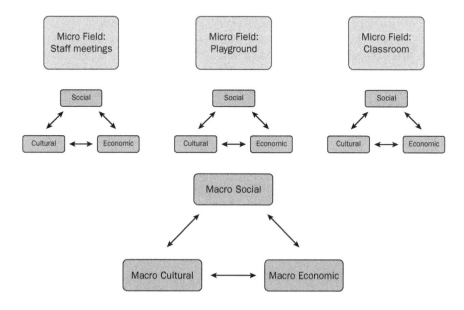

**Figure 7.2**   Macro and micro fields and their capitals

## Ofsted Framework

### Cultural capital

204. As part of making the judgement about the quality of education, inspectors will consider the extent to which schools are equipping pupils with the knowledge and cultural capital they need to succeed in life. Our understanding of 'knowledge and cultural capital' is derived from the following wording in the national curriculum.

It is the essential knowledge that pupils need to be educated citizens, introducing them to the best that has been thought and said and helping to engender an appreciation of human creativity and achievement.

(Ofsted, 2021a)

### Quality of education

Inspectors will make judgement on the quality of education by evaluating the extent to which:

### Intent

- leaders take on or construct a curriculum that is ambitious and designed to give all learners, particularly the most disadvantaged and those with special educational needs and/or disabilities (SEND) or high needs, the knowledge and cultural capital they need to succeed in life
- the provider's curriculum is coherently planned and sequenced towards cumulatively sufficient knowledge and skills for future learning and employment
- the provider has the same academic, technical or vocational ambitions for almost all learners. Where this is not practical – for example, for some learners with high levels of SEND – its curriculum is designed to be ambitious and to meet their needs
- learners study the full curriculum. Providers ensure this by teaching a full range of subjects for as long as possible, 'specialising' only when necessary

(Ofsted, 2021b)

of free will or the structures, rather it's the child of the interplay of both. There is no decree absolute of how a senior leader will act in a staff meeting, playground or in a classroom. There are no fixed rules around what the teacher wears, but we all know that rules and etiquettes exist.

Isabel Wilkerson gives a personal example of observing the habitus in action while on a trip to India researching the Dalit class by stating she:

began to be able to tell who was the high born and who was low born among the Indian people among us, not from what they looked like, as one might when in the United States, but on the basis of the universal human response to hierarchy, in the case of an upper caste person an inescapable certitude in bearing, demeanour, behaviour, a visible expectation of centrality. (Wilkerson, 2020)

I assume that the Ofsted framework (2021) means that schools should be equipping students with a schematic repertoire to navigate society. This is fine; teaching students how to make choices that make them more 'successful' is not controversial. 'The best that has been thought and said' and 'an appreciation of human creativity and achievement' need the addition of 'by those imbued with whiteness' and 'of whiteness' to be truly authentic. Now in each micro field, let's ask whose cultural capital is of value? Whose unwritten rules and structural expectancies are held as worthy? In the playground, whose games are catered for? Whose norms are adhered to? In the classroom, the poetry of Shakespeare has more value than Rumi, the Rza, or Chip. Why is this? Is it the aesthetics? The content? The 'nature' of the language?

## Is This about Knowledge?

Let's think about the educational canon in schools; what is the decision makers' cultural capital? The culture they accept and propagate? Power begets power, and the habitus begets, well, more habitus. Why do certain groups cluster together in the playground and tend to behave in similar ways? In staff meetings, why do Teachers of Colour rarely feel comfortable wearing traditional garments? Who decides where value resides in your organisation? Is 'value' a synonym for how entrenched in whiteness the cultural activities are?

The etiquette of 'business wear' style uniforms is more important than the students' expressions of self in the classroom's micro field. These different sections of society all have different levels of value. Through teaching a pre-selected narrative, we impose our political views on the children we serve. I have no issue with being political; after all, all teaching as well as being and acts of the arts and knowing are all simultaneously an act of politics (Freire, 1985).

However, what happens when we elevate one culture over another? The cultural capital of BAME groups, no matter how valuable, if not aligned with whiteness is deemed worthless. Students of Colour are forced to adapt by rejecting that part of themselves, forced to navigate this discord constantly. The process presents as subconscious code-switching between social groups, home and school; this is exhausting, taking up precious cognitive resources, leading to many issues. It begs the question, is this about knowledge or is this about protecting the status quo? We are trained through our education system to endorse this ideology by promoting a particular type of knowledge and actively denigrating the global majority's cultural worth through the denigration of their knowledge. Forms of art such as hip hop, graffiti, and street dance are not accepted because they are not born of whiteness. Thus we do not choose to teach certain topics because they are inherently the best, but because they are deemed so by a small group of people in power who wish to perpetuate a certain type of knowledge and 'Britishness'.

## The Altar of Success

In the real world, society's macro field is a culmination of the cultural capitals that become the status quo. In everything we see, these norms and behaviours are reinforced. Whiteness and anything with proximity to it are good, and everything else is relegated to playing a subservient role. Those with monetary resources may gain social connections to fit in more readily into the existing habitus of success (swapping economic and social capital for cultural capital). For this exchange to happen, people may wilfully deny the canon of Colour either externally in overt expression of denying its worth or internally through a subconcious rejection of one's heritage.

Remember, the three capitals and sources of power are interchangeable. If the colour of your cultural capital pot is too dark, you either have to start a new barrel in exchange for either economic and social capital or accept that this society is not for you. This is where dissonance and separation occurs, where Students of Colour start to exclude parts of themselves in order to engage and/or internalise the impact of racism.

'To thine own self be true', Polonius exclaims to his son, intending to advise Laertes on behaving at university in act 1 scene 3 of Shakespeare's *Hamlet*. I would have to agree if 'thine' own self has not had to be battered and moulded into the accepted model.

The world, your teachers and those who are successful constantly reinforce the message to students that 'white knowledge is good, everyone else's is bad.' Racism in its internalised form turns the victims of oppression (People of Colour) into the perpetrators of further injustice through a process called defensive othering. Fanon takes this ever deeper and describes sub-oppression in *Black Skin, White Masks*. Remember, this exhibition of internalised racism comes straight from societal training. This is the habitus; these are the rules of the game. Upon the altar of success, Students of Colour are forced to sacrifice their heritage, identity and parts of themselves in return for potentially getting ahead and being recognised as worthy by their teachers.

## Habitus Is Self-protecting and Propagating

Any habitus is self-replicating and self-propagating. Capoeira is a Brazilian martial art forged during the oppression of slavery. Due to the need for the secretive nature of martial arts training under enslavement, certain rules were developed to protect its practitioners (or players) from the ire of the authorities:

1. Capoeira is always played to music.
2. Players practise in a circle (roda).
3. The roda is entered by the berimbau.
4. The music dictates the pace and flow of the game.
5. When and if a chamada (call) is made, there are rules about the next engagement.

Other than the above, the game is played in any way you'd like: cartwheels left and right, head spins, whatever you can conceive of as long as the structure holds. Over the last two centuries, capoeira has evolved through various schools of thought, regional, angola, and contemporary. No matter what capoeiristas produce, it is always variations of the same brand. Bourdieu refers to these rules as doxa. In the same way as capoeira uses these norms of engagement, doxa ensures the habitus reproduces differing versions of itself.

## To Be Human Is to Create

Music, fine art, and dance have existed in every corner of the globe since the dawn of time. To create is to be human. People are excluded from 'scholarship' and the beauty of human endeavour because they lack the funds, knowledge of norms and connections. We have come full circle, back to Bourdieu's three capitals. Earlier I quoted Polonius from Shakespeare's *Hamlet*: 'To thine own self be true', but you have to be exposed to the actual play to appreciate the nature of the speech. We have a man who is extolling the virtue of freedom that his son should live by; he is a blatant hypocrite, later spying on, and interfering in the lives of both of his children to the point that his daughter chooses suicide. All the while, his children see him as being an object of ridicule, as they are often seen standing out of his sightline mocking him through physical gestures.

When social strata or any group are not able to appreciate the approved art due to the lack of time, money or contacts, it becomes challenging to discuss and learn to understand the work of Rembrandt or Dickens. People not only miss out, but they are unlikely ever to be able to consume and engage. How does one access any of these pots, let alone exchange?

When there is no place for 'us', the only thing left to do is to create. Create your own. Alternative modern cultural capitals are formed instead; for example, graffiti instead of fine art, spoken word for poetry and rap (or in the UK grime) for classical music. However, these tranches never make it into the curriculum, they never receive that kind of approval.

## The Impact – Categorisation?

People's brains form categories of what success looks like based on the associations they make. Let us look at leadership being a measure of success. Leadership associations are born of repeatedly seeing the same attributes linked to tangible measures such as leadership positions and status. What your brain thinks a successful leader looks like can influence your perception of the leader regardless of their actions or merits. Rosette et al. (2008) asked undergraduates to read a newspaper article about an interview with either a leader or an employee from a business; the dependent variable was the manipulation of the racial composition of the organisation (either 50% or 20% white).

If racialised leadership prototypes were present and influenced participants' perceptions, the expected result would be that the leaders would be assumed to be white regardless of the company's racial make-up. Even if whites were a minority of the workforce, they would still be more likely to be leaders than workers. We assume that white people are much more likely to be thought of as the standard for leaders in both cases. And indeed leaders were perceived to be white more frequently than employees regardless of the racial composition. They went on to study and conclude that the white leadership prototype holds regardless of business industry and that white leaders are evaluated better after success. Finally, white leaders are seen as having better career prospects than global majority leaders.

## What Is Success? Who Is Seen as Successful?

Earlier, in Chapter 2 on teacher bias, we discussed personal construct theory. Success is an example of a personal construct; this means it will have different meanings depending on who is defining it. Archer (2008) suggests that teachers simultaneously define success in four categories: 'traditional' academic success; 'good enough' success; 'value-added' success; and 'desired-denied'/'potential' success. She does not aim for the definitions to be fixed or exhaustive but uses the descriptions as a way of mapping out broad educational discourse.

Through a similar process described by Fiske et al. (2002), Archer argues that educational 'success' in the eyes of teachers is very much an 'impossible' subjective position for minority ethnic students. She states that: '[O]nly White, middle-class students – but particularly boys – could enjoy an unproblematised association with "traditional" academic success' (Archer, 2008, p. 23). This is due to the academic position that Merton (1948) explains: that even when minoritised groups are successful, they are seen as doing so in the wrong way (too passive, worked too hard, etc.). Success in students is viewed through the lens of a particular model and thus ethnic minority students are racialised, gendered and or classed, and as a consequence idealised, othered or demonised (Archer, 2008).

What are the standard prototypes for success? White, middle-class, cis, hetero, etc. These groups are often misrecognised and idealised as being in possession of traits – such as innovative, assertive, leaders, enquiring, engaging – not by their qualifications or achievements. Inversely it is also true that we position 'demonised' pupils as challenging because they are seen to be owners of those immutable traits of success, but in a negative way (e.g. lacking ability, peer-led, anti-social, ungovernable, aggressive). Is success attributed and not achieved in our eyes (Bourdieu and Waquant 1992, in Archer 2008)?

## Pigeonholing

As a Person of Colour, the habitus can also hold you to stereotypes, which negatively impacts on you and the world around you. Teachers of Colour are often pigeonholed into roles in which society sees us as fit for and this means that many of us conform to succeed. I have spent my career being told I should be leading pastoral roles although my CV may not necessarily reflect that.

When the (unwritten) rules tell you that to be successful you must behave in a certain way, then to be your authentic self becomes an act of resistance; to even have a voice or a story becomes an act of rebellion. Your very existence is a choice between the worlds you traverse. To acquiesce or live a life of bondage to a world that is not nor never will be yours.

Recently there have been a number of People of Colour being placed into diversity roles within schools. Despite having lived experience, they are not given the time in their workloads or support from the school to implement changes. Melanin is not necessarily a precursor to skills and knowledge, and like every facet of school improvement, these roles are in need of investment in terms of time and money.

---

**ACTIVITY**

Go to YouTube and search for the late Chadwick Boseman's speech addressing a graduating class of his alma matter (Howard University). It describes an interaction with an executive producer who hired him. Reflect upon how he was pigeonholed here. How do you think pigeonholing plays out within an educational setting? Do you see Colleagues of Colour being pigeonholed when it comes to championing and discussing diversity and inclusion?

---

Up to this point this chapter has been based around recognising the structures of whiteness around us. Those structures are the water we drink and the air we breathe. Your students may incorporate these into themselves just like we have. What happens when students arrive in your classroom with problematic opinions? How do we allow them to flourish in their expression of thought and have the the skills to differentiate between racism or any other extreme view that they are taught through our society?

## Burn the Books

Before we talk about pedagogy we need to establish the positionality of the teacher and their students. Every one of us has a journey and this idea of equality is a farce. As an individual I need to recognise the Brown man (my position in society) is different to Black, melanated and white students. I must realise that from my perspective, experiences may seem very different to that of the students we teach. There is no objective truth when it comes to social perspective. There is no right or wrong.

We all bring to the table a legacy of different experiences. All experiences have value. We can't begin to talk about critical thinking until we appreciate that a young person's experiences are equally as valid as our own. Remember that we are the protagonists of our own lives; whether we like it or not, everything we do is centred around our perspective. Acknowledging our position in society and establishing positionality is the first step. The education system as it stands upholds an unequal society and disadvantages some people while lifting others up. Giving pupils the tools to access this world of success around them is not contentious. The omission of the reality of the power structures is where there are real issues. How do we teach our students and ourselves to become more critical of the world around us? From the content we teach to the plethora of information in wider society, we are bombarded constantly.

A common response in schools to a racist comment would be 'You can't say that! You can't think or say that, those views must not be expressed in class. That's a sanction! Go to the Headteacher!'. If we push at students' views the likelihood is that we will encourage resistance; nobody likes to be told they are wrong and this act of banning forces the practice underground where it can grow unchecked. Our aim is to facilitate a self-interrogation; raising consciousness around what was said and why will allow students to gain an understanding of what they are saying and how it might hurt another. We can't ignore them or ban them. When we challenge any views, it is not about agreement, disagreement or any type of fealty, it's that we are interested in the thought pattern here and what brought them to this point. If you have created a culture in which all children are prepared to question and be questioned, you are facilitating them in being able to question all the power structures around them and not just take things at face value.

## What is a Critical Learning Community? In Conversation with James Nottingham

Many teachers may feel ill equipped to have conversations around race, and that is how racism enters our classrooms through a lack of the mechanisms and tools to have these conversations. If a critical culture of enquiry has been built, the learning community will successfully debunk and squash any apparent prejudice regardless of teacher intervention.

The word critical comes from the Greek word 'kritikos' which can be translated to 'being able to make a judgement' and philosophy comes from the roots of the love of knowledge. There is a misconception that criticality can be taught in the moment. This has to be built over time; the time is needed to learn and teach the strategies involved around critical thought. The community then needs to gain traction to build up a wisdom around critical thought.

Classrooms are built through a sense of community and trust, criticality, shared language understanding and experience. It is important for educators to recognise that teaching critical thinking strategies or structures does not in itself create a sense of wisdom. For wisdom to evolve, there must be the inclusion of the human element in the conversation, which includes the positionality of the parties involved.

## Exemplar Cause and Effect

This is a common strategy in which students are encouraged and taught to be able to identify causes and effects in scenarios in text or in speech. Students may become adept at picking out and inferring meaning from situations. In science we can easily see this being taught in the teaching of homeostasis and the process of hunger and replenishment, or in history in the origins of the First World War and arguably the Second World War. Cause and effect can be taught through a solely positivist (an absolute) lens: the war was caused because of the assassination of Archduke Franz Ferdinand, which had a consequential effect on the Second World War, and onwards, etc., but this does nothing to teach students about the human element. What did those interactions mean to the people involved and what do they mean to the receivers of that knowledge now? In classrooms a common technique is to run through the different perspectives of cause and effect. This strategy is particularly pertinent in teaching through an antiracist lens as listening to different reasoning points towards positionality, e.g. the teaching of colonialism may land differently on the descendants of the coloniser and the colonised peoples.

## What Is a Critical Thinking Argument?

In critical terms an argument is a **conclusion** supported by **reasons** that are intended to **persuade**.

## Examples

**(1) 'We should be at the station by 11 o'clock because the train leaves at 11:10.'**
This is not really an argument, as although there is a conclusion and a reason, there was no persuasive element to it. To make this more of a critical argument we add:

> As we don't want to be rushed, if we miss that train the next one is an
> hour away, that ticket is the cheapest – so make sure you're there on time.

This leads to the obvious path of teaching students to break down and either support or resist everything put in front of them. Students should be able to ask and identify:

> What is the conclusion?
> What are the reasons?
> What is the agenda?

**(2) 'Institutional racism does not exist because we have looked into it and we have concluded that it doesn't.'**
A conclusion exists in the above statement: 'Institutional racism doesn't exist'. The critical arguments are lacking in their entirety and that is even

---

## ACTIVITY: Critical Thinking

For this activity I provide an excerpt of an interview between Sophie Ridge and Matt Hancock on diversity within the cabinet:

> S: How many Black people are in the cabinet?
> M: Erm, Well... there is a whole series of people from a Black and minority background, the chancellor of the exchequer, the home secretary to name but two.
> S: Sorry, I am talking about Black people specifically. I do think it is important to not lump everyone from non-white backgrounds together because obviously Asian people face prejudice too but it might be a different prejudice faced by Black people...

I want you to think critically by asking yourself the following questions:

1.  What is the critical question/conclusion?
2.  Do the reasons match the conclusion?
3.  What is the agenda of the source of the reasons?

---

before we look at any possible agendas. Asking the simple questions of the folx putting forward the argument:

Who are they?
What do they believe?
Why are they trying to persuade me?

**In the classroom children may have views like**: 'Girls can't play football.' Rather than shutting down this kind of belief with 'you shouldn't say that, this is sexist', we should help facilitate the student's critical thinking to understand how they came to this conclusion, to help them learn from the interaction. Look at this as a critical learning moment:

Student: Girls can't play football.
Teacher: Why do you think this?
Student: Well my sister can't play football.
Teacher: But that is just one girl, this doesn't mean all girls can't play football.

Now is the time to question:

Teacher: What are you really good at?
Student: Cricket.

Teacher: Are all boys good at cricket?
Student: No, he (points to another boy) hates cricket.

Here, you can educate the student that gender has nothing to do with being good or bad at something. Rather, each person has strengths and weaknesses, or enjoys one thing over another.

Racism is built on sand; there are no foundations whatsoever. In fact all oppression which is based on innate characteristics is an accumulation of rhetoric and prejudice; there is no critical thinking behind any of it at all. In the case of children, we do not want this child not to express what is in his head. We want it out in the open to help him knock down his sand-castle of prejudice, and hiding his voice actually fortifies it. Remember the aim is to teach children to think for themselves, and using the framework sets them up to do that. We must endeavour to ensure an environment where thought can flourish. The critical classroom has these attributes:

1.  We will listen.
2.  We will say what we think.
3.  We will expect everything to be questioned.
4.  We will expect no one to say 'no, you're right'.
5.  We will expect everyone to ask why, why is that, could you explain that a bit more, who would put that view across?

But … does it still apply if we have children who bring racist views into the room? Do we still want to give those children the opportunity to speak, give them a platform to address their peers? As an educator what would you do? I believe that a sanction, sending them to the person in authority or shutting them down will not have the same impact. If we have created a critical environment the class themselves will question the absurdity of the statement and break down the non-consequential nature of the statement and interrogate the agenda of the children and adults portraying those ideologies.

Providing students with the tools to recognise, promote and even challenge racism in our society is not political. Well, maybe it is. But, how is not teaching pupils to recognise and critique the world around us not a political act? Does that not leave them at the mercy of those who seek to manipulate them without the tools to protect themselves and differentiate? Leaving young people to enter the world without those skills is damaging surely. Whether we teach the skills to critically evaluate and then democratically resist or promote what they fundamentally believe or not. Act or not, teach or omit, do or do not, all are acts of politics.

## Conclusion

The root of power in the context of racism lives with the epistemology (the way knowledge is accepted) and our actions as educators and leaders.

We must as educators look at the positions that we inhabit relative to the students in our care and seek to interrogate the value in the content we teach, and give our pupils the skills to traverse society and act in a manner that serves them. It is important to accept that very few things in education are quick fixes; in teaching power we should recognise the safe and brave space cannot be created in a silo and on the spot. Antiracism and classroom communities have to be nurtured into questioning environments which prepare our young people for life in today's society.

## Chapter Takeaways

- Accept that you are privileged by virtue of being a teacher in a classroom. Think about the other characteristics you own and how that interplay colours your interactions with your students.
- Consider what you and the curriculum see as having value. What is the best that has ever been thought and said? And what is your metric?
- Foster an environment where questioning is the norm, where all views are heard and interrogated.

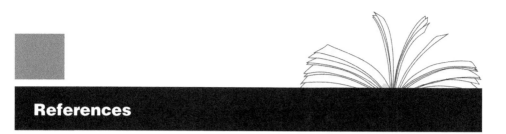

# References

## Chapter 1

Di Angelo, R. (2011). White fragility. *International Journal of Critical Pedagogy*, 3(3): 54–70.

Foner, P. S. (Ed.) (1999). *Frederick Douglass: Selected Speeches and Writings*. Abridged and adapted by Y. Taylor. Chicago: Lawrence Hill Books.

Higher Education Statistics Agency (HESA) (2021). Who's working in HE? Personal characteristics. HESA. Available at: www.hesa.ac.uk/data-and-analysis/staff/working-in-he/characteristics [accessed 26 August 2021].

Keates, C. (2021). *Visible Minorities, Invisible Teachers*. Runnymedetrust.org. Available at: www.runnymedetrust.org/invisibleteachers.html [accessed 28 July 2021].

Kendi, I. X. (2019). *How to Be an Antiracist*. New York: One World.

Rush, D. (2021). *Pyramid of White Supremacy' Draws Controversy at SU*. Available at: www.delmarvapublicmedia.org/post/pyramid-white-supremacy-draws-controversy-su [accessed 6 November 2021].

## Chapter 2

Adams, R. (2020). Fewer than 1% of UK university professors are Black, figures show. The *Guardian*. Available at: www.theguardian.com/education/2020/feb/27/fewer-than-1-of-uk-university-professors-are-black-figures-show [accessed December 2020].

Allen, G. and Kirk-Wade, E. (2020). Terrorism in Great Britain: The statistics. House of Commons Brefing Paper CB7613, 26 March. Available at: https://researchbriefings.files.parliament.uk/documents/CBP-7613/CBP-7613.pdf [accessed 22 November 2021].

Allport, G. W. (1954). *The Nature of Prejudice*. Boston, MA: Addison-Wesley.

Aronson, J., Quinn, D. M. and Spencer, S. J. (1998). Stereotype threat and the academic underperformance of minorities and women. In J. K. Swim and C. Stangor (Eds.), *Prejudice: The Target's Perspective* (pp. 83–103). Cambridge, MA: Academic Press.

Beasley, M. A. and Fischer, M. J. (2012). Why they leave: The impact of stereotype threat on the attrition of women and minorities from science, math and engineering majors. *Social Psychology of Education*, 15: 427–448.

Blascovich, J., Spencer, S. J., Quinn, D. M. and Steele, C. M. (2001). African Americans and high blood pressure: The role of stereotype threat. *Psychological Science*, 12(3): 225–229.

Campbell, T. (2015). Stereotyped at seven? Biases in teacher judgement of pupils' ability and attainment. *Journal of Social Policy*, 44(3): 517–547. doi: 10.1017/S0047279415000227.

Carter, S. P., Honeyford, M., McKaskle, D., Guthrie, F., Mahoney, S. and Carter, G. (2007). 'What do you mean by whiteness?' A professor, four doctoral students, and a student affairs administrator explore whiteness. *College of Students Affairs Journal*, 26(2): 152–159.

Cheryan, S. and Bodenhausen, G. V. (2000). When positive stereotypes threaten intellectual performance: The psychological hazards of 'model minority' status. *Psychological Science*, 11(5): 399–402. doi: 10.1111/1467-9280.00277.

Chung, B. G. et al. (2010). Stereotype threat, state anxiety, and specific self-efficacy as predictors of promotion exam performance. *Group & Organization Management*, 35(1): 77–107. doi: 10.1177/1059601109354839.

Cohen, G. L., Garcia, J., Purdie-Vaughns, V., Apfel, N. and Brzustoski, P. (2009). Recursive processes in self-affirmation: Intervening to close the minority achievement gap. *Science*, 324(5925): 400–403. doi: 10.1126/science.1170769.

Curtis, C. P. (1957). *A Commonplace Book*. New York: Simon & Schuster.

Dearden, L. (2021). More white people arrested over terrorism than any other ethnic group for third year in a row. *Independent*, 4 March. Available at: www.independent.co.uk/news/uk/crime/terrorism-arrests-uk-white-ethnic-b1812288.html [accessed 22 November 2021].

Feagin, J. R. (2010). *The White Racial Frame: Centuries of Racial Framing and Counter-Framing*. New York: Routledge.

Fiske, S. T. (2018). Stereotype content: Warmth and competence endure. *Current Directions in Psychological Science*, 27(2): 67–73. doi: 10.1177/09637214 17738825.

Goyer, P., Garcia, J., Purdie-Vaughns, V., Binning, K., Cook, J., Reeves, S., Apfel, N., Taborsky-Barba, S., Sherman, D. and Cohen, G. (2017). Self-affirmation facilitates minority middle schoolers' progress along college trajectories. *Proceedings of the National Academy of Sciences of the United States of America*. Available at: https://doi.org/10.1073/pnas.1617923114 [accessed 22 November 2021].

Harackiewicz, J. M., Canning, E. A., Tibbetts, Y., Giffen, C. J., Blair, S. S, Rouse, D. I. and Hyde, J. S. (2014). Closing the social class achievement gap for first-generation students in undergraduate biology. *Journal of Educational Psychology*, 106(2): 375–389. doi: 10.1037/a0034679.

Hecht, A., Priniski, S. J. and Harackiewicz, J. M. (2019). Understanding long-term effects of motivation interventions in a changing world. In E. N. Gonida and M. S. Lemos (Eds.), *Motivation in Education at a Time of Global Change* (*Advances in Motivation and Achievement*, Vol. 20). Bingley: Emerald

Publishing Limited, pp. 81–98. https://doi.org/10.1108/S0749-742320190000020005.

Hilton, J. L. and von Hipple, W. (1996). Stereotypes. *Annual Review of Psychology*, 47: 237–271.

Johns, M., Inzlicht, M. and Schmader, T. (2008). Stereotype threat and executive resource depletion: Examining the influence of emotion regulation. *Journal of Experimental Psychology, General*, 137(4): 691–705. https://doi.org/10.1037/a0013834.

Levin, D. T. and Banaji, M. R. (2006). Distortions in the perceived lightness of faces: The role of race categories. *Journal of Experimental Psychology, General*, 135(4): 501–512.

McGarty, C., Yzerbyt, V. Y. and Spears, R. (2002). *Stereotypes as Explanations: The Formation of Meaningful Beliefs about Social Groups*. Cambridge: Cambridge University Press.

MacLin, O. H. and Malpass, R. S. (2001). Racial categorization of faces: The ambiguous race face effect. *Psychology, Public Policy, and Law*, 7(1): 98–118. https://doi.org/10.1037/1076-8971.7.1.98.

MacLin, O. H. and Malpass, R. S. (2003). The ambiguous-race face illusion. *Perception*, 32(2): 249–252. doi:10.1068/p5046.

MacLin, M. K, MacLin, O. H. and Malpass, R. S. (2001). Using the implicit association test to assess ambiguous race faces. Paper presented at the 2001 Convention of the Rocky Mountain Psychological Association, Reno, NV, USA, April 2001.

Martens, A., Johns, M., Greenberg, J. and Schimel, J. (2006). Combating stereotype threat: The effect of self-affirmation on women's intellectual performance. *Journal of Experimental Social Psychology*, 42(2): 236–243. https://doi.org/10.1016/j.jesp.2005.04.010.

Mendes, W. B. and Jamieson, J. (2012). Embodied stereotype threat: Exploring brain and body mechanisms underlying performance impairments. Oxford Scholarship Online. doi: 10.1093/acprof:oso/9780199732449.003.0004.

Mills, C. (1997). *The Racial Contract*. Ithaca, NY: Cornell University Press.

Miyake, A., Kost-Smith, L. E., Finkelstein, N. D., Pollock, S. J., Cohen, G. L. and Ito, T. A. (2010). Reducing the gender achievement gap in college science: A classroom study of values affirmation. *Science*, 330(6008): 1234–1237. doi: 10.1126/science.1195996.

Schmader, T. and Hall, W. M. (2014). Stereotype threat in school and at work: Putting science into practice. *Policy Insights from the Behavioral and Brain Sciences*, 1(1): 30–37. doi: 10.1177/2372732214548861.

Schmader, T. and Johns, M. (2003). Converging evidence that stereotype threat reduces working memory capacity. *Journal of Personality and Social Psychology*, 85(3): 440–452.

Shapiro, J. R., Williams, A. M. and Hambarchyan, M. (2013). Are all interventions created equal? A multi-threat approach to tailoring stereotype threat interventions. *Journal of Personality and Social Psychology*, 104(2): 277–288.

Sherman, D. K and Cohen, G. L. (2006). The psychology of self-defense: Self-affirmation theory. *Advances in Experimental Social Psychology*, 38: 183–242. https://doi.org/10.1016/S0065-2601(06)38004-5.

Shih, M., Pittinsky, T. and Ambady, N. (1999). Stereotype susceptibility: Identity salience and shifts in quantitative performance. *Psychological Science*, 10: 80–83.

Sibley, C. G. and Osborne, D. (2015). *Stereotype*. Wiley Online Library. https://doi.org/10.1002/9781118541555.wbiepc096.

Steele, C. M. (1997). A threat in the air: How stereotypes shape the intellectual identities and performance. *American Psychologists*, 52: 612–639.

Steele, C. M. and Aronson, J. (1995). Stereotype threat and the intellectual test performance of African Americans. *Journal of Personality and Social Psychology*, 69(5): 797–811.

Steele, C. M., Spencer, S. J. and Aronson, J. (2002). Contending with group image: The psychology of stereotype and social identity threat. In: M. P. Zanna (Ed.), *Advances in Experimental Social Psychology*, vol. 34. London: Academic Press, pp. 379–440. www.sciencedirect.com/sdfe/pdf/download/eid/1-s2.0-S0065260102800090/first-page-pdf.

Taylor, V. J. and Walton, G. M. (2011). Stereotype threat undermines academic learning. *Personality and Social Psychology Bulletin,* 37(8): 1055–1067. doi: 10.1177/0146167211406506.

Von Mises, L. (2003). The group vs. the collective. In: *Epistemological Problems of Economics*, 3rd edition. Auburn, AL: Ludwig von Mises Institute.

Walton, G. M. and Cohen, L. G. (2003). Stereotype lift. *Journal of Experimental Social Psychology*, 39(5): 456–467.

# Chapter 3

Ackerman, J. M., Shapiro, J. R., Neuberg, S. L., Kenrick, D. T., Vaughn Becker, V. D., Griskevicius, V., Maner, J. K. and Schaller, M. (2006). They all look the same to me (unless they're angry): From out-group homogeneity to out-group heterogeneity. *Psychological Science*, 17(10): 836–840. doi: 10.1111/j.1467-9280.2006.01790.x.

Allport, G. W. (1945). The basic psychology of rumor. *Transactions of the New York Academy of Sciences*, Series, II, VIII (pp. 61–81).

Anderson, E. (1999). *Code of the Street: Decency, Violence, and the Moral Life of the Inner City*. New York: W.W. Norton & Company.

Bargh, J. A. and Chartrand, T. L. (1999). The unbearable automaticity of being. *American Psychologist*, 54(7): 462–479. https://doi.org/10.1037/0003-066X.54.7.462.

Berkowitz, L. (1984). Some effects of thoughts on anti- and prosocial influences of media events: A cognitive-neoassociation analysis. *Psychological Bulletin*, 95(3): 410–427. https://doi.org/10.1037/0033-2909.95.3.410.

Blake, J. and Epstein J. D. R. (2019). End adultification bias. YouTube.com. Available at: www.youtube.com/watch?v=L3Xc08anZAE [accessed 29 January 2021.]

Boon, J. C. and Davis, G. M. (1987). Rumours greatly exaggerated: Allport and Postman's apocryphal study. *Canadian Journal of Behavioural Science /*

*Revue canadienne des sciences du comportement*, 19(4): 430–440. https://doi.org/10.1037/h0079995.

Casas, A. (2017). Black girls 'perceived as less innocent'. BBC News. Available at: www.bbc.co.uk/news/av/world-us-canada-40451554 [accessed 29 January 2021].

Clark, R., Benkert, R. and Flack, J. (2006). Large arterial elasticity varies as a function of gender and racism-related vigilance in Black youth. *Journal of Adolescent Health*, 39: 562–569. doi: 10.1016/j.jadohealth.2006.02.012.

Coker, T. R., Elliott, M. N., Toomey, S. L. et al. (2016). Racial and ethnic disparities in ADHD diagnosis and treatment. *Pediatrics*, 138(3). doi: 10.1542/peds.2016-0407.

Cottrell, C. A. and Neuberg, S. L. (2005). Different emotional reactions to different groups: A sociofunctional threat-based approach to prejudice. *Journal of Personality and Social Psychology*, 88(5): 770–789. https://doi.org/10.1037/0022-3514.88.5.770.

Devine, P. G. (1989). Stereotypes and prejudice: Their automatic and controlled components. *Journal of Personality and Social Psychology*, 56(1): 5–18. https://doi.org/10.1037/0022-3514.56.1.5.

Du Bois, W. E. B. (1903). *The Souls of Black Folk: Essays and Sketches*. Chicago: A. C. McClung.

Duncan, B. L. (1976). Differential social perception and attribution of intergroup violence: Testing the lower limits of stereotyping of Blacks. *Journal of Personality and Social Psychology*, 34(4): 590–598. https://doi.org/10.1037/0022-3514.34.4.590.

Earp, B. D. (2010). Automaticity in the classroom: Unconscious mental processes and the racial achievement gap. *Journal of Multiculturalism in Education*, 6(1): 1–22.

Eberhardt, J. L., Goff, P. A., Purdie, V. J. and Davies, P. G. (2004). Seeing black: Race, crime, and visual processing. *Journal of Personality and Social Psychology*, 87(6): 876–893. https://doi.org/10.1037/0022-3514.87.6.876.

Epstein, R., Blake, J. and González, T. (2017). *Girlhood Interrupted: The Erasure of Black Girls' Childhood*. Georgetown Law Center. Available at: https://genderjusticeandopportunity.georgetown.edu/wp-content/uploads/2020/06/girlhood-interrupted.pdf [accessed 29 January 2021].

Fadus, M. C., Ginsburg, K. R., Sobowale, K. et al. (2020). Unconscious bias and the diagnosis of disruptive behavior disorders and ADHD in African American and Hispanic youth. *Academic Psychiatry*, 44: 95–102. https://doi.org/10.1007/s40596-019-01127-6.

Gorman–Smith, D. and Tolan, P. (1998). The role of exposure to community violence and developmental problems among inner-city youth. *Development and Psychopathology*, 10(1): 101–116. doi: 10.1017/S0954579498001539.

Halberstadt, A. G., Castro, V. L., Chu, Q., Lozada, F. T. and Sims, C. M. (2018). Teachers' racialized emotion recognition, anger bias, and hostility attributions. *Contemporary Educational Psychology*, 54: 125–138. http://dx.doi.org/10.1016/j.cedpsych.20.

Hicken, M. T., Lee, H., Ailshire, J., Burgard, S. A. and Williams, D. R. (2013). 'Every shut eye, ain't sleep': The role of racism-related vigilance in racial/

ethnic disparities in sleep difficulty. *Race and Social Problems*, 5: 100–112. doi: 10.1007/s12552-013-9095-9.

Himmelstein, M. S., Young, D. M., Sanchez, D. T. and Jackson, J. S. (2015). Vigilance in the discrimination-stress model for Black Americans. *Psychology & Health*, 30(3): 253–267. https://doi.org/10.1080/08870446.2014.966104.

Hopkins, K. (2011). Associations between police-recorded ethnic background and being sentenced to prison in England and Wales. Ministry of Justice. Available at: https://assets.publishing.service.gov.uk/government/uploads/system/uploads/attachment_data/file/479874/analysis-of-ethnicity-and-custodial-sentences.pdfhttp://www.nationalarchives.gov.uk/doc/open-government-licence/version/1/open-government-licence.htm [accessed 14 December 2020].

Hopkins, K., Uhrig, N. and Colahan, M. (2015). Associations between ethnic background and being sentenced to prison in the Crown Court in England and Wales in 2015. Ministry of Justice. Available at: https://assets.publishing.service.gov.uk/government/uploads/system/uploads/attachment_data/file/568896/associations-between-ethnic-background-being-sentenced-to-prison-in-the-crown-court-in-england-and-wales-2015.pdf [accessed 14 December 2020].

Hugenberg, K. and Bodenhausen, G. V. (2003). Facing prejudice: Implicit prejudice and the perception of facial threat. *Psychological Science*, 14(6): 640–643. doi: 10.1046/j.0956-7976.2003.psci_1478.x.

Kahneman, D. (2011). *Thinking, Fast and Slow*. New York: Farrar, Straus and Giroux.

Kendall, M. (2021). *Hood Feminism: Notes from the Women White Feminists Forgot*. London: Bloomsbury.

Knuf, L., Aschersleben, G. and Prinz, W. (2001). An analysis of ideomotor action. *Journal of Experimental Psychology: General*, 130: 779–798. doi: 10.1037/0096-3445.130.4.779.

Levin, D. T. and Banaji, M. R. (2006). Distortions in the perceived lightness of faces: The role of race categories. *Journal of Experimental Psychology: General*, 135(4): 501–512.

Maner, J. K., Kenrick, D. T., Becker, D. V., Robertson, T. E., Hofer, B., Neuberg, S. L., Delton, A. W., Butner, J. and Schaller, M. (2005). Functional projection: How fundamental social motives can bias interpersonal perception. *Journal of Personality and Social Psychology*, 88(1): 63–78. https://doi.org/10.1037/0022-3514.88.1.63.

Merton, R. (1948). The self-fulfilling prophecy. *Antioch Review*, 8(2): 193–210. doi:10.2307/4609267.

Mischel, W. and Shoda, Y. (1995). A cognitive-affective system theory of personality: Reconceptualizing situations, dispositions, dynamics, and invariance in personality structure. *Psychological Review*, 102(2): 246–268. doi:10.1037/0033-295X.102.2.246.

Morgan, P. L., Staff, J., Hillemeier, M. M., et al. (2103). Racial and ethnic disparities in ADHD diagnosis from kindergarten to eighth grade. *Pediatrics*, 132(1): 85–93.

Payne, B. K. (2001). Prejudice and perception: The role of automatic and controlled processes in misperceiving a weapon. *Journal of Personality and Social Psychology*, 81(2): 181–192. https://doi.org/10.1037/0022-3514.81.2.181.

Richardson, H. (2019). Black pupils' schooling 'dumbed down over special needs'. BBC News. Available at: https://www.bbc.co.uk/news/education-47240580 [accessed 1 August 2021].

Saad, L. (2020). *Me and White Supremacy: How to Recognise Your Privilege, Combat Racism and Change the World*. London: Quercus.

Sagar, H. A. and Schofield, J. W. (1980). Racial and behavioral cues in Black and White children's perceptions of ambiguously aggressive acts. *Journal of Personality and Social Psychology*, 39(4): 590–598. https://doi.org/10.1037/0022-3514.39.4.590.

Shoda, Y., Mischel, W. and Wright, J. C. (1994). Intraindividual stability in the organization and patterning of behavior: Incorporating psychological situations into the idiographic analysis of personality. *Journal of Personality and Social Psychology*, 67(4): 674–687.

Stewart, E. A., Schreck, C. J. and Simons, R. L. (2006). 'I ain't gonna let no one disrespect me': Does the code of the street reduce or increase violent victimization among African American adolescents? *Journal of Research in Crime and Delinquency*, 43(4): 427–458. doi: 10.1177/0022427806292338.

Strand, S. and Lindorff, A. (2018). Ethnic disproportionality in the identification of Special Educational Needs (SEN) in England: Extent, causes and consequences. Available at: http://www.education.ox.ac.uk/wp-content/uploads/2018/08/Executive-Summary_2018-12-20.pdf [accessed 12 August 2021].

Weisbuch, M., Pauker, K. and Ambady, N. (2009). The subtle transmission of race bias via televised nonverbal behavior. *Science*, 326(5960): 1711–1714. doi: 10.1126/science.1178358.

Williams, D. R. and Mohammed, S. A. (2009). Discrimination and racial disparities in health: Evidence and needed research. *Journal of Behavioral Medicine*, 32: 20–47. doi: 10.1007/s10865-008-9185-0.

Wilson, A. N. (1978). *The Developmental Psychology of the Black Child*. New York, NY: Afrikan World InfoSystems.

Zajonc, R. B., Pietromonaco, P. and Bargh, J. A. (1982). Independence and interaction of affect and cognition. In M. S. Clark and S. T. Fiske (Eds.), *Affect and Cognition: The Seventeenth Annual Carnegie Symposium on Cognition* (pp. 211–228). Hillsdale, NJ: Erlbaum.

# Chapter 4

Alvidrez, J. and Weinstein, R. S. (1999). Early teacher perceptions and later student academic achievement. *Journal of Educational Psychology*, 91(4): 731–746. https://doi.org/10.1037/0022-0663.91.4.731.

Angelou, M. (1982). *The Heart of a Woman*. New York: Bantam.

Archer, L., Francis, B., Miller, S., Taylor, B., Tereshchenko, A., Mazenod, A., Pepper, D. and Travers, M.-C. (2018). The symbolic violence of setting: A Bourdieusian analysis of mixed methods data on secondary students' views about setting. *British Educational Research Journal*, 44(1): 119–140.

Babad, E., Bernieri, F. and Rosenthal, R. (1989). Nonverbal communication and leakage in the behavior of biased and unbiased teachers. *Journal of Personality and Social Psychology*, 56(1): 89–94. https://doi.org/10.1037/0022-3514.56.1.89.

Babad, E., Bernieri, F. and Rosenthal, R. (1991). Students as judges of teachers' verbal and nonverbal behavior. *American Educational Research Journal*, 28(1): 211–234. doi: 10.3102/00028312028001211.

Bandura, A. (1977). Self-efficacy: Toward a unifying theory of behavioral change. *Psychological Review*, 84(2): 191–215.

Bandura, A. (1986). *Social Foundation of Thought and Action: A Social Cognitive Theory*. Englewood Cliffs, NJ: Prentice-Hall.

Bandura, A. (1993). Perceived self-efficacy in cognitive development and functioning. *Educational Psychologist*, 28(2): 117–148, doi: 10.1207/s15326985ep2802_3.

Bandura, A. (1997). *Self-efficacy: The Exercise of Control*. New York: Freeman.

Benjamin, L. T. J. (2009). The birth of American intelligence testing. *Monitor on Psychology*, 40(1). www.apa.org/monitor/2009/01/assessment

Boaler, J. (1997). Setting, social class and survival of the quickest. *British Educational Research Journal*, 23(5): 575–595.

Boaler, J. (2005). The 'psychological prisons' from which they never escaped: The role of ability grouping in reproducing social class inequalities. *Forum*, 47(2): 135–144. http://doi.org/10.2304/forum.2005.47.2.2.

Burgess, S. and Greaves, E. (2009). *Test Scores, Subjective Assessment and Stereotyping of Ethnic Minorities*. Centre for Market and Public Organisation, University of Bristol. Available at: www.bristol.ac.uk/media-library/sites/cmpo/migrated/documents/wp221.pdf [accessed November 2020].

Campbell, T. (2015). Stereotyped at seven? Biases in teacher judgement of pupils' ability and attainment. *Journal of Social Policy*, 44(3): 517–547. doi: 10.1017/S0047279415000227.

Connolly, P., Taylor, B., Francis, B., Archer, L., Hodgen, J., Mazenod, A. and Tereshchenko, A. (2019). The misallocation of students to academic sets in maths: A study of secondary schools in England. *British Educational Research Association*, 45: 873–897. https://doi.org/10.1002/berj.3530.

Demie, F. and Strand, S. (2006). English language acquisition and attainment in secondary schools. *Educational Studies*, 32: 215–231. doi: 10.1080/03055690600631119.

Dodge, K. A. (2006). Translational science in action: Hostile attributional style and the development of aggressive behavior problems. *Development and Psychopathology*, 18(3): 791–814. doi: 10.1017/S0954579406060391.

Fasfous, A., Hidalgo-Ruzzante, N., Vilar-Lopez, R., Catena-Martinez, A. and Perez-Garcia, M. (2013). Cultural differences in neuropsychological abilities required to perform intelligence tasks. *Archives of Clinical Neuropsychology*, 28(8): 784–790.

Fiske, S. (2002). What we know about bias and intergroup conflict, the problem of the century. *American Psychological Society*, 11(4): 123–128. https://journals.sagepub.com/doi/pdf/10.1111/1467-8721.00183.

Hvidman, U. and Sievertsen, H. (2021). High-stakes grades and student behavior. *Journal of Human Resources*, 56: 821–849. doi: 10.3368/jhr.56.3.0718-9620R2.

Johnston, R., Wilson, D. and Burgess, S. (2004). School segregation in multiethnic England. *Ethnicities*, 4(2): 237–265. doi: 10.1177/1468796804042605.

Jussim, L., Coleman, L. M. and Lerch, L. (1987). The nature of stereotypes: A comparison and integration of three theories. *Journal of Personality and Social Psychology*, 52(3): 536–546. doi: 10.1037/0022-3514.52.3.536.

Keating, K. (2019). 11 things we know about marking and 2 things we don't… yet. Ofqual Blog. Available at: https://ofqual.blog.gov.uk/2019/03/05/14572/ [accessed 26 August 2021].

Madon, S., Jussim, L. and Eccles, J. (1997). In search of the powerful self-fulfilling prophecy. *Journal of Personality and Social Psychology*, 72(4): 791–809. https://doi.org/10.1037/0022-3514.72.4.791.

Marks, R. (2011). 'Ability' ideology and its consequential practices in primary mathematics. *Proceedings of the British Society for Research into Learning Mathematics*, 31(2): 43–48.

Marks, R. (2013). 'The blue table means you don't have a clue': the persistence of fixed-ability thinking and practices in primary mathematics in English schools, *Forum: For Promoting 3–19 Comprehensive Education*, 55(1): 31–44.

Merton, R. (1948). The self-fulfilling prophecy. *Antioch Review*, 8(2): 193–210. doi: 10.2307/4609267.

Muijs, D. and Dunne, M. (2010). Setting by ability – or is it? A quantitative study of determinants of set placement in English secondary schools. *Educational Research*, 52(4): 391–407. doi: 10.1080/00131881.2010.524750.

Nunes, T., Bryant, P., Sylva, K. and Barros, R. (2009) *Development of Maths Capabilities and Confidence in Primary School*. In collaboration with ALSPAC, University of Bristol. Research Report No. DCSF-RR118. University of Oxford.

Rosenthal, R. and Babad, E. Y. (1985). Pygmalion in the gymnasium. *Educational Leadership* 43(1): 36–39.

Rosenthal, R. and Jacobson, L. (1968). *Pygmalion in the Classroom: Teacher Expectation and Students' Intellectual Development*. New York: Holt, Rinehart & Winston.

Slavin, R. E. (1990). Achievement effects of ability grouping in secondary schools: A best-evidence synthesis. *Review of Educational Research*, 60(3): 471–499.

Social Metrics Commission (2020). Measuring poverty. Available at: https://socialmetricscommission.org.uk/wp-content/uploads/2020/06/Measuring-Poverty-2020-Web.pdf [accessed 27 August 2021].

Spear, R. C. (1994). Teacher perceptions of ability grouping practices in middle level schools. *Research in Middle Level Education*, 18(1): 117–130. doi: 10.1080/10825541.1994.11670041.

Wilson, D., Burgess, S. and Briggs, A. (2011). The dynamics of school attainment of England's ethnic minorities. *Journal of Population Economics*, 24: 681–700. https://doi.org/10.1007/s00148-009-0269-0.

Yaeger, D. S., Purdie-Vaughns, V., Garcia, J., Apfel, N., Brzustoski, P., Master, A., Hessert, W. T. and William M. E. (2013). Breaking the cycle of mistrust: Wise interventions to provide critical feedback across the racial divide. *Journal of Experimental Psychology*, 143(2): 804–824.

# Chapter 5

Abramson, L. Y., Seligman, M. E. and Teasdale, J. D. (1978). Learned helplessness in humans: Critique and reformulation. *Journal of Abnormal Psychology*, 87(1): 49–74. https://doi.org/10.1037/0021-843X.87.1.49.

Alloy, L. B., Abramson, L. Y., Metalsky, G. I. and Hartlage, S. (1988). The hopelessness theory of depression: Attributional aspects. *British Journal of Clinical Psychology*, 27(1): 5–21.

Bandura, A. (1977). Self-efficacy: Toward a unifying theory of behavioral change. *Psychological Review*, 84: 191–215.

Bernard, D. L., Calhoun, C. D., Banks, D. E. et al. (2020). Making the 'C-ACE' for a culturally-informed adverse childhood experiences framework to understand the pervasive mental health impact of racism on Black youth. *Journal of Child Adolescent Trauma*, 14: 233–247. https://doi.org/10.1007/s40653-020-00319-9.

Cave, L., Cooper, M. N., Zubrick, S. R. and Shepherd, C. C. J. (2020). Racial discrimination and child and adolescent health in longitudinal studies: A systematic review. *Social Science & Medicine*, 250: 112864. https://doi.org/10.1016/j.socscimed.2020.112864.

Christian, L. M. (2012). Psychoneuroimmunology in pregnancy: Immune pathways linking stress with maternal health, adverse birth outcomes, and fetal development. *Neuroscience & Biobehavioral Reviews*, 36(1): 350–361. https://doi.org/10.1016/j.neubiorev.2011.07.005.

Davis, E. P. and Sandman, C. A. (2006). Prenatal exposure to stress and stress hormones influences child development. *Infants & Young Children*, 19(3): 246–259.

Dweck, C. S., Davidson, W., Nelson, S. and Enna, B. (1976) Sex differences in learned helplessness: (II) The contingencies of evaluative feedback in the classroom and (III) An experimental analysis. Unpublished manuscript, University of Illinois at Urbana-Champaign.

Felitti, V. J., Anda, R. F., Nordenberg, D., Williamson, D. F., Spitz, A. M., Edwards, V., Koss, M. P. and Marks, J. S. (1998). Relationship of childhood abuse and household dysfunction to many of the leading causes of death in adults. The Adverse Childhood Experiences (ACE) Study. *American Journal of Preventive Medecine*, 14(4): 245–58. https://doi.org/10.1016/S0749-3797(98)00017-8.

Gershenson, S., Hart, C. M. D., Hyman, J., Lindsay, C. A. and Papageorge, N.W. (2018). The long-run effects of same-race teachers. Available at: https://voxeu.org/article/long-run-effects-same-race-teachers [accessed 13 August 2021].

Glass, D. C., Singer, J. E. and Friedman, L. N. (1969). Psychic cost of adaptation to an environmental stressor. *Journal of Personality and Social Psychology*, 12(3): 200–210. https://doi.org/10.1037/h0027629.

Glass, D. C., Reim, B. and Singer, J. R. (1971). Behavioral consequences of adaptation to controllable and uncontrollable noise. *Journal of Experimental Social Psychology*, 7: 244–257.

Gov.UK (2020). School workforce in England. Available at: https://explore-education-statistics.service.gov.uk/find-statistics/school-workforce-in-england [accessed 24 November 2021].

Hilmert, C. J., Dominguez, T. P., Schetter, C. D., Srinivas, S. K., Glynn, L. M., Hobel, C. J. and Sandman, C. A. (2014). Lifetime racism and blood pressure changes during pregnancy: Implications for fetal growth. *Health Psychology*, 33(1): 43–51. https://doi.org/10.1037/a0031160.

Himmelstein, M. S., Young, D. M., Sanchez, D. T. and Jackson, J. S. (2015). Vigilance in the discrimination-stress model for Black Americans. *Psychology & Health*, 30(3): 253–267. https://doi.org/10.1080/08870446.2014.966104.

Holt, S. and Gershenson, S. (2017). The Impact of Teacher Demographic Representation on Student Attendance and Suspensions. IZA Discussion Paper No. 9554. Available at SSRN: https://ssrn.com/abstract=2708367 [accessed 24 November 2021].

Houtepen, L. C., Heron, J., Suderman, M. J., Fraser, A., Chittleborough, C. R. and Howe, L. D. (2020). Associations of adverse childhood experiences with educational attainment and adolescent health and the role of family and socioeconomic factors: A prospective cohort study in the UK. *PLoS Med*, 17(3): e1003031. https://doi.org/10.1371/journal.pmed.1003031.

Hughes, K., Bellis, M. A., Hardcastle, K. A., Sethi, D., Butchart, A., Mikton, C., Jones, L. and Dunne, M. P. (2017). The effect of multiple adverse childhood experiences on health: A systematic review and meta-analysis. *Lancet Public Health*, 2(8): e356–e366. doi: 10.1016/S2468-2667(17)30118-4. Epub 2017 Jul 31. PMID: 29253477.

Iyengar, U., Kim, S., Martinez, S., Fonagy, P. and Strathearn, L. (2014). Unresolved trauma in mothers: Intergenerational effects and the role of reorganization. *Frontiers in Psychology*, 5(5). https://doi.org/10. 3389/fpsyg.2014.00966.

James, W. (1890). *The Principles of Psychology*. London: Macmillan.

Jones, K. P., Peddie, C. I., Gilrane, V. L., King, E. B. and Gray, A. L. (2016). Not so subtle: A meta-analytic investigation of the correlates of subtle and overt discrimination. *Journal of Management*, 42(6): 1588–1613. https://doi.org/10.1177/0149206313506466.

Kirkinis, K., Pieterse, A. L., Martin, C., Agiliga, A. and Brownell, A. (2018). Racism, racial discrimination, and trauma: A systematic review of the social science literature. *Ethnicity & Health*, 26(3): 1–21. doi:10.1080/13557858.2018.1514453.

Lê-Scherban, F., Wang, X., Boyle-Steed, K. H. and Pachter, L. M. (2018). Intergenerational associations of parent adverse childhood experiences and child health outcomes. *Pediatrics*, 14(6), e20174274. https://doi.org/10.1542/peds.2017-4274.

Letourneau, N., Dewey, D., Kaplan, B. J., Ntanda, H., Novick, J., Thomas, J. C., Deane, A. J., Leung, B., Pon, K., Giesbrecht, G. F. and the APrON Study Team (2019). Intergenerational transmission of adverse childhood experiences via maternal depression and anxiety and moderation by child sex. *Journal of Developmental Origins of Health and Disease*, 10(1): 88–99. https://doi.org/10.1017/ S2040174418000648.

Lindsay, C. A. and Hart, C. M. D. (2017). Teacher race and school discipline: Are students suspended less often when they have a teacher of the same race?. *Education Next*, 17(1). Available at: https://link.gale.com/apps/doc/A474717812/AONE?u=anon~3d0cdca1&sid=googleScholar&xid=93e178b3 [accessed 8 August 2021].

Maier, S. F. and Seligman, M. E. (1976). Learned helplessness: Theory and evidence. *Journal of Experimental Psychology: General*, 105(1): 3–46. https://doi.org/10.1037/0096-3445.105.1.3.

Malon, D. (2021). Restorative justice practices in Tribal Courts. Pine Tree Legal Assistance. Available at: www.ptla.org/wabanaki/restorative-justice-practices-tribal-courts [accessed 8 August 2021].

Meulewaeter, F., De Pauw, S. S. W. and Vanderplasschen, W. (2019). Mothering substance use disorders and intergenerational trauma transmission: An attachment-based perspective. *Frontiers in Psychiatry*, 10. https://doi.org/10.3389/fpsyt.2019.00728.

Miller, P. W. (2020). 'Tackling' race inequality in school leadership: Positive actions in BAME teacher progression – evidence from three English schools. *Educational Management Administration & Leadership,* 48(6): 986–1006. doi: 10.1177/1741143219873098.

Nepomnaschy, P. A., Welch, K. B., McConnell, D. S., Low, B. S., Strassmann, B. I. and England, B. G. (2006). Cortisol levels and very early pregnancy loss in humans. *Proceedings of the National Academy of Sciences*, 103(10): 3938–3942. https://doi.org/10.1073/pnas.0511183103.

Priest, N., Paradies, Y., Trenerry, B., Truong, M., Karlsen, S. and Kelly, Y. (2013). A systematic review of studies examining the relationship between reported racism and health and wellbeing for children and young people. *Social Science & Medicine*, 95: 115–127. https://doi. org/10.1016/j.socscimed .2012.11.031.

Racine, N., Palmondon, A., Madigan, S., McDonald, S. and Tough, S. (2018). Material adverse childhood experiences and infant development. *Pediatrics*, 14(4), e20172495. https://doi.org/10.1542/peds.2017-2495.

Redmond, B. F. (2010). Self-efficacy Theory: Do I think that I can succeed in my work? *Work Attitudes and Motivation*. The Pennsylvania State University, World Campus.

Tereshchenko, A., Mills, M. and Bradbury, A. (2020). *Making progress? Employment and retention of BAME teachers in England*. [online] London: UCL, p.3. Available at: https://discovery.ucl.ac.uk/id/eprint/10117331/1/IOE_Report_BAME_Teachers.pdf [accessed 27 October 2021].

Weininger, R. and Kearney, M. (2011). Revisiting empathic engagement: Countering compassion fatigue with 'Exquisite Empathy'. In I. Renzenbrink (Ed.), *Caregiver Stress and Staff Support in Illness, Bereavement and Dying*. New York: Oxford University Press.

Williams, D. R. (1997). Race and health: basic questions, emerging directions. *Annals of Epidemiology*, 7: 322–333.

Williams, D. R. and Collins, C. (2001). Racial residential segregation: A fundamental cause of racial disparities in health. *Public Health Reports,* 116: 404–416.

Williams, D. R, Lawrence, J. A., and Davis, B. A. (2019a). Racism and health: Evidence and needed research. *Annual Review of Public Health,* 40(1): 105–125.

Williams, D., Lawrence, J., Davis, B. and Vu, C. (2019b). Understanding how discrimination can affect health. *Health Services Research*, 54 Suppl. 2. doi: 10.1111/1475-6773.13222.

Vygotsky, L. S. (1978). *Mind in Society: The Development of Higher Psychological Processes*. Cambridge, MA: Harvard University Press.

# Chapter 6

Adichie, C. (2021). The danger of a single story. Ted.com. Available at: https://www.ted.com/talks/chimamanda_ngozi_adichie_the_danger_of_a_single_story?language=en [accessed 8 August 2021].

Baldwin, J. (1972). *No Name in the Street*. London: Michael Joseph.

BBC News (2013). Mau Mau torture victims to receive compensation – Hague. 6 June. Available at: https://www.bbc.co.uk/news/uk-22790037 [accessed 8 September 2021].

Chaudhuri, B., Chakrabarti, S. and Patnaik, U. (2019). *Agrarian and Other Histories*. New Delhi: Tulika Books.

Chetty, D. (2019). Darren Chetty at 'The Thriving Child'. Available at: www.youtube.com/watch?v=BpqHC19tFvI&t=62s [accessed 13 September 2021].

CLPE (2020). Reflecting Realities: *Survey of Ethnic Representation within UK Children's Literature* 2019. Available at: https://clpe.org.uk/research/clpe-reflecting-realities-survey-ethnic-representation-within-uk-childrens-literature [accessed 24 November 2021].

Counsell, C. (2018). Senior Curriculum Leadership 1: The indirect manifestation of knowledge: (A) Curriculum as narrative. Christine Counsell's Blog. Available at: https://thedignityofthethingblog.wordpress.com/2018/04/07/senior-curriculum-leadership-1-the-indirect-manifestation-of-knowledge-a-curriculum-as-narrative/ [accessed December 2020].

Dahlgreen, W. (2014). The British Empire is 'something to be proud of'. Available at: https://yougov.co.uk/topics/politics/articles-reports/2014/07/26/britain-proud-its-empire [accessed 26 July 2014].

Fanon, F. (1965). *The Wretched of the Earth*. New York: Grove Press, Inc.

Hammond, K. (2014). Building and assessing historical knowledge on three scales. Historical Association. Available at: www.history.org.uk/publications/resource/8133/building-and-assessing-historical-knowledge-on-thr [accessed 13 July 2021].

Lakshmi, R. (2015). What did Mahatma Gandhi think of black people? Available at: www.washingtonpost.com/news/worldviews/wp/2015/09/03/what-did-mahatma-gandhi-think-of-black-people [accessed 24 November 2021].

Padesky, C. (1994). Schema change processes in cognitive therapy. *Clinical Psychology & Psychotherapy,* 1(5): 267–278.

Piaget, J. (1976). Piaget's theory. In B. Inhelder, H. H. Chipman and C. Zwingmann (Eds.) *Piaget and His School*. Springer Study Edition. Berlin, Heidelberg: Springer. https://doi.org/10.1007/978-3-642-46323-5_2.

Shukla, N. (ed.) (2017). *The Good Immigrant*. London: Unbound.

Tharoor, S. (2017). *Inglorious Empire*. London: C. Hurst & Co.

Thomas, D. (2017). Oscar-nominated 'Hidden Figures' was whitewashed – but it didn't have to be. 25 January. Available at: www.vice.com/en/article/d3xmja/ oscar-nominated-hidden-figures-was-whitewashed-but-it-didnt-have-to-be [accessed 8 September 2021].

Twiselton, S. (2002). *Beyond the Curriculum: Learning to Teach Primary Literacy*. PhD thesis, University of Birmingham.

# Chapter 7

Abbott, J. (1994). *Learning Makes Sense: Re-creating Education for a Changing Future*. Letchworth: Education 2000.

Archer, L. (2008). The impossibility of minority ethnic educational 'success'? An examination of the discourses of teachers and pupils in British secondary schools. *European Educational Research Journal*, 7(1): 89–107. doi: 10.2304/ eerj.2008.7.1.89.

Baldwin, James (1962). As much truth as one can bear. *New York Times*, 14 January.

BMA (2021). Race inequalities and ethnic disparities in healthcare. Available at: www.bma.org.uk/advice-and-support/nhs-delivery-and-workforce/workforce/ race-inequalities-and-ethnic-disparities-in-healthcare [accessed 17 August 2021].

Bergsieker, H. B, Leslie, L. M., Constantine, V. S. and Fiske, S. T. (2012). Stereotyping by omission: Eliminate the negative, accentuate the positive. *Journal of Personality and Social Psychology*, 102: 1214–1238.

Black, S. and Allen, J. D. (2018). Part 5: Learning is a social act. *The Reference Librarian*, 59(2): 76–9. doi: 10.1080/02763877.2017.1400932.

Bourdieu, P. and Wacquant, L. (1992). *An Invitation to Reflexive Sociology*. Chicago: University of Chicago Press.

Carnell, E. and Lodge, C. (2002). *Supporting Effective Learning*. London: PCP National School Improvement Network.

Fanon, F. (1967). *Black Skin, White Masks*. New York: Grove.

Fiske, S. T. (2002). What we know now about bias and intergroup conflict, the problem of the century. *Current Directions in Psychological Science*, 11(4): 123–128. doi: 10.1111/1467-8721.00183.

Fiske, S.T. (2015). Intergroup biases: A focus on stereotype content. *Current Opinion in Behavioral Sciences*, 3: 45–50.

Fiske, S. T. (2018). Stereotype content: Warmth and competence endure. *Current Directions in Psychological Science*, 27(2): 67–73. doi: 10.1177/09637214177 38825.

Fiske, S. T., Cuddy, A. J. C., Glick, P. and Xu, J. (2002). A model of (often mixed) stereotype content: Competence and warmth respectively follow from perceived status and competition. *Journal of Personality and Social Psychology*, 82(6): 878–902.

Freire, P. (1972). *The Pedagogy of the Oppressed*. New York: Herder and Herder.

Freire, P. (1985). Reading the world and reading the word: An interview with Paulo Freire. *Language Arts*, 62(1): 15–21. Available at: www.jstor.org/stable/41405241.

Horton, M. and Freire, P. (1990). *We Make the Road by Walking*. Philadelphia: Temple University Press.

Lee, T. L. and Fiske, S. T. (2006). Not an outgroup, not yet an ingroup: Immigrants in the stereotype content model. *International Journal of Intercultural Relations*, 30(6): 751–768. https://doi.org/10.1016/j.ijintrel.2006.06.005.

Leonardo, Z. (2004). The color of supremacy: Beyond the discourse of 'white privilege'. *Educational Philosophy and Theory*, 36(2): 137–152. doi: 10.1111/j.1469-5812.2004.00057.x.

Merton, R. (1948). The self-fulfilling prophecy. *Antioch Review*, 8(2): 193–210. doi:10.2307/4609267.

Ofsted (2021a). *School Inspection Handbook*. Available at: www.gov.uk/government/publications/school-inspection-handbook-eif/school-inspection-handbook [accessed 15 September 2021].

Ofsted (2021b). Education Inspection Framework. Available at: www.gov.uk/government/publications/education-inspection-framework/education-inspection-framework [accessed 14 September 2021].

Rosette, A., Leonardelli, G. and Phillips, K. (2008). The white standard: Racial bias in leader categorization. *Journal of Applied Psychology*, 93: 758–777. doi: 10.1037/0021-9010.93.4.758.

Summers, H. (2021). Black women in the UK four times more likely to die in pregnancy or childbirth. *The Guardian* 15 January. Available at: www.theguardian.com/global-development/2021/jan/15/black-women-in-the-uk-four-times-more-likely-to-die-in-pregnancy-or-childbirth [accessed 24 November 2021]

Wilkerson, I. (2020). *Caste*. London: Allen Lane.

# Index